THE
JOURNEYS
OF
EDITH BOON

The Journeys Of Edith Boon

by

Barbara Haigh

Central Publishing Limited
West Yorkshire

Paperback ISBN 1 903970 32 6

Published
by
Central Publishing Limited
Royd Street Offices
Royd Street
Huddersfield
West Yorkshire
HD3 4QY

www.centralpublishing.co.uk

Acknowlededgments

Many thanks must go to Edith's friends for their help in producing this book.

Special thanks to:

Anne Townsend and Jean Marland who inherited Edith's personal effects and freely gave me her notes, scrapbooks and maps and assisted with personal memories.

Jack Kirkbride for us of the cartoon.

Philip Hurst, editor of the Oldham Chronicle for the use of the articles from the paper.

Enid Michael, photojournalist, for access to her files of photos, and her permission to use them.

CONTENTS

Dedication
The Journeys. An introduction
Hints on planning a long distance journey on horseback
Bridleways past and present: A plea
"Dobcross To Dodworth." 1948
"Around Skipton." 1950
"Exploring The Local Pennines By Packhorse Roads." 1950
"Round The Peak." 1951
"From Saddleworth To The Severn Country." 1952
"Yorkshire Dales And The North Yorkshire Moors." 1957
"Shrewsbury Circle." 1961
"Lancashire And Yorkshire." 1964
"North Yorkshire Journey To The East Coast." 1964
"To Dovedale In Derbyshire." 1976
"Northumberland And Durham." 1977
"Yorkshire Dales And Fells." 1978
"Through The Yorkshire Dales." 1978
"The Great Triangle." 1979
Article for "The Hostelling News." By Edith Boon
"James Herriot's Yorkshire." 1980
"Yorkshire Journey." 1982
"The Great Circle." 1983
"Cornwall." 1984
"Across Yorkshire." 1985
"The Lake District."
"Dunford Bridge Circular." 1998
"Shrewsbury Circle Revisited." 1997
"Hadrian's Wall Revisited." 1997
An Article For The British Horse Society. By Edith Boon

Dedicated to Edith, who was an inspiration to many.

Acknowledgements

Many thanks must go to Edith's friends for their help in producing this book. Especial thanks to

ANN TOWNSEND and JEAN MARLAND who inherited Edith's personal effects and freely gave me her notes, scrapbooks and maps, and assisted with personal memories.

JACK KIRKBRIDE for the use of the cartoon.

PHILLIP HURST, editor of the Oldham Chronicle, for the use of the articles from the paper.

ENID MICHAEL, photojournalist, for access to her files of photos, and her permission to use them.

THE JOURNEYS
An Introduction

Prior to Edith's death I held long discussions with her about the routes she used between overnight stops, and recorded her actual route for the first half of her 70th birthday 770-mile ride, with a view to writing them up at a later date.

Due to her experiences of blocked or overgrown bridleways, her preferred routes were 'white roads', rather than bridleways. The use of these roads also meant that she met interesting people and went through pretty villages. She was not unduly concerned by traffic, as both Simon and later Sam were both traffic-trained horses.

Wherever possible I have used the routes Edith used, bridleways in areas she knew or when travelling with a local rider, 'white roads' at other times.

Barbara Haigh

HINTS ON PLANNING A LONG DISTANCE JOURNEY ON HORSEBACK.

These journeys are definitely pleasurable and educational rides; they are not competitive, nor are they tests of endurance. Other riders making similar journeys set out with definite ideas about the route to be followed, but hope to find suitable accommodation en route. This I will not do, however short or long the journey. I arrange detailed accommodation so that I know where I am to lay my head each night, and where my mount is to rest and feed.

PLANNING

The period of the year must always be May to September so that the horse may be left out at night if necessary. Rest days, too, need to be organised.

I first decide how much time is to be spent and the area to be visited. I then consult the YHA map of the British Isles, which shows all the hostels. These are often within one day's walking distance of each other. Where the distance is more than one day, I investigate the possibility of finding a friend or relative living nearby who can help. If I am unlucky, I consult the local Tourist Information and guidebooks for guest houses etc.

Now the route begins to take shape. Once I have definite ideas about night stops, I make a list of dates on a sheet of foolscap leaving sufficient space to enter details of accommodation.

ACCOMMODATION (Self and Horse)

Now the real work begins. With suitable maps around me I start on the difficult detailed writing for bed, breakfast and evening meal. Where the accommodation is at a Youth Hostel, money must be sent in advance and wardens asked to supply the name and address of a nearby farmer or stables on the back of the receipt. I then write to the recommended person myself. Occasionally the Hostel has a paddock, but it is wise to make sure this is well fenced (this is not the case as a rule). Friends and relatives can hopefully supply information of local farmers or stables and guest houses, too, can be asked to co-operate by supplying information about stabling or a field.

MONEY

Villages with a bank must be visited at times- in my own case I also arrange to be near a Post Office on Thursdays- pension day!!

WASHING FACILITIES

Post Offices interest me for another reason. Whilst still fairly near home I post soiled linen to a good friend, who washes it quickly and sends it to an address I've written on the inside of the wrapping paper. This scheme has only failed me once (when the post office was on strike in 1979) and it took a while for the parcel post to run smoothly again. I have a prearranged plan for sending and receiving these parcels (see also note under Gear (maps) below).

I use three sets of clothes, one on and two in the post.

Further afield, I find launderettes, or my hostesses have had washers and dryers.

GEAR

Self: - I ride in rubber riding boots (fields are wet in the mornings even in dry weather) and I have a quilted jacket and a shower-proof cape with hood (carried in the front of the saddle).

In my PANNIERS I carry toiletries (minimum), night wear, 3/4 days underwear, shirts, socks, a pair of slacks for evening and a pair of sandals (not much more than soles).

All material MUST be crush proof. Polythene bags are invaluable.

Horse: - A waterproof bag containing hoof pick, grooming kit (minimum), head collar and certain spares of saddlery (eg. spare girth) This I carry at the back of the saddle.

All tack MUST be examined before setting out for weaknesses in the paddinq and stitching.

A REAL SHEEPSKIN numnah is advisable or a REAL woollen blanket, folded.

MAPS

One cannot carry the numerous maps necessary. I arrange for maps to be sent by post to where they will be required (exact planning needed here) and the envelope containing the map holds a stamped addressed envelope in which to return the map no longer needed. This process is expensive, but the smooth running makes the cost worthwhile.

BLACKSMITH

You may well be asking, 'What about a blacksmith?' You need to be constantly alert to this need and if a blacksmith is handy, shoes must be replaced even if not worn out.   If you are staying with 'horsey' friends they will call in their own blacksmith. If I come across a blacksmith at a riding school, I'm first in the queue as I have to be off! Early!

FIRST AID KIT   for horse and me.

NOTE: *OS maps show bridleways, BUT these are often blocked.*

EDITH BOON

Barbara Haigh

BRIDLEWAYS PAST AND PRESENT
A PLEA

Comments relative to the production of new maps, on which essential bridleways will be defined (1978).

Many of the routes the British Horse Society and the Bridleways Association wish to claim for riders of the future are labelled on old maps as LANES – which may be:

a. Tracks fenced on both sides   or
b. Unfenced, on uncultivated non-pasture uplands.

These lanes, or green roads, have a remarkable history. They have been "highways" of importance, and were a vital part of the economic system of their time. Some were prehistoric links between hut settlements and Iron Age sites. Some were of Roman origin, long and straight, ignoring local needs. The Pack Horse Roads were directly linked with the economic and social life of their time.

Packhorses or ponies were the prime form of transport for approximately five centuries, largely developed in monastic times. Monasteries spread their economy over wide areas; by packhorse roads they moved wood, coal, iron, lead, charcoal, peat, corn, fish and many other supplies.

Drovers moved hundreds of head of sheep and cattle along the Drove Roads; and spent weeks on their journeys, resting at Inns where there was also suitable grazing.

Salt was another prime necessity moved from the sea-coast – Cheshire or South Lancashire – across the Pennines on these green lanes.

After the Dissolution of the Monasteries they still remained in use, connecting villages with peat allotments, hill pastures, lead and coal mines etc. Eventually, the traffic shifted into the valleys; Turnpike Trusts were set up. They widened tracks and bridges and set up new roads more level and more suitable for wheeled vehicles. Folks travelling by horseback could be landowners visiting property, tenants visiting Manorial Courts, monastic servants etc.

In our own area, all these historical facts are illustrated, plus a very close and intimate feature – the old routes were extensively used by wool Broggers – the collectors and distributors of wool for home spinning and weaving. Local historian Ammon Wrigley tells us of this in his book, "Rakings Up". Even his mother used the lanes of the Castleshaw area, riding horseback, straddle-legged! She would carry a bolt (enough for a suit) of woollen cloth to take to Huddersfield to find a buyer. Ammon, himself, drove his newly wed wife (a Marsden girl) in a horse and trap from Diggle Station to Oxhey. He used the old tracks over Harrop Edge, across Castleshaw Valley, up the hillside and across Broadhead Noddle.

In view of the aforementioned facts, it would seem easy to return all the lanes, (unfit for motorised vehicles) to the horse and its rider, defining them as Bridleways. (No need for evidence forms, anyway, the vast number of witnesses is now, sadly, out of our reach!!!)

This is a sport, which can be catered for very cheaply – the only expense would be the re-installing of the drainage system here and there. Farmers could be encouraged to keep their walls and fences in good order, and cease the practice of blocking the green lanes to stop their animals from straying.

EDITH BOON

"Dobcross To Dodworth"
1948

To spend four days away from home on a hiking or cycling trip is not uncommon, but an equestrian 'trip' is perhaps a little more rare, so that the following account may be of interest to the general public, and (we hope) the horseman. It deals with a ride from Dobcross to Dodworth (a village near Barnsley in Yorkshire), an approximate distance of thirty miles, which took place over a September weekend.

It was a mixed group of seven riders that moved from Mrs. Edith Boon's Riding School, Burnedge Lane at 10:15 a.m. on Saturday, September 11th. The leader was Mrs. Edith Boon, who together with Miss Peggie Ownsworth and Miss Irene Lord had mapped out the journey and partly surveyed it on foot some time previously. The first part of the route lay over Lark Hill, a once reputed Highwayman's haunt in the days when a long journey on horseback was a risky venture. The absence of bushes on each side of the track is said to have indicated that measures were taken to discourage any would-be Dick Turpin from springing out of cover.

Having cantered over Lark Hill, a short trotting session on the Standedge Road was followed by a short cut over Black Moss Moor and so on to the Marsden Road, where after a welcome sip of coffee at the Hare and Hounds we settled down to a two mile walk into Marsden before turning off to go through Wessenden Valley. Most people will know of Marsden's association with the old packhorse track, which runs northwest from Marsden over an ancient bridge, and emerges on the Huddersfield – Denshaw Road. The ride through Wessenden was one of the highlights of the trip. Many local people, both cyclists and hikers, will be familier with this valley containing some of the Huddersfield Corporation Water Works. The track hangs mostly on steep hillsides descending sharply to narrow wooden bridges. Riding over such ground is quite thrilling, but I would advise the nervously inclined to look strictly in front of them.

At Wessenden Lodge we attacked and demolished a substantial lunch, and then on to the well-known Isle of Sky Inn, the fourth highest In England. After a brief halt there - to rest the horses - we started off on the last stage of the day's journey to Dunford Bridge, through Austonley and Holm Bridge. An outstanding feature of this stage was the remarkable view from Cook's Study. On the downward track the horses were quick to realize that they were nearing the end of' the day's ride, to all of them it was new country, and yet before reaching the Stanhope Arms where we were to stay the night, we could scarcely hold them back, and they rushed into the inn yard.

Dunford Bridge itself, judged by scenic standards, is rather uninteresting; remarkable only for its Railway Station, where apparently the only activity takes place at night under one's bedroom window.

Until now, the weather had been good, but the deluge started early on Sunday morning, holding off only long enough for us to groom and saddle our mounts. Under any other circumstances the day's ride through Carlecotes, Thurlstone and Penistone, to Dodworth, would have been depressing, but such was the spirit of the party that everyone seemed to find it highly amusing. It was even alleged that one member of the party nearly fell off his horse with laughter. On arrival at Hods Farm, Dodworth we were soon out of our soaking garments and drying in front of a large fire. Fortunately, Sunday was the only wet day, and our macs were not needed until our return to Oldham.

On leaving the farm our return route was much the same, and we renewed acquaintance with many people we had met on the outward journey. Our main diversion was a delightful ride through the woods adjoining Home Farm - although much of the surrounding country was showing the desolation left by open cast mining.

On leaving Marsden we enjoyed a good two-mile canter over the moor and so to tea at Bleak Hey Nook, after which we regretfully turned for home to end a four-day holiday packed with interest. By seven p.m. We were back at the riding school, unsaddling for the last time and feeling much more competent horsemen in every way.

Naturally, in this short account, much has been left out, as every day was full of' incident .The horses, for instance, behaved marvellously, and tackled some very difficult country to the manner born. We also had our fair share of humour; for example, on one occasion our humorist Mr. Ron Mellor found himself perched rather precariously on his horse at the bottom of a fairly tricky gulley, while the rest of the party, having successfully negotiated it, were all yelling instructions to him. Mrs Raymond Redfern, having done some riding in the foothills of the Himalayas, would have been quite happy to charge madly over hill and dale, which naturally occasioned some criticism from the riding mistress.

To sum up, I should like to say to people who imagined that riding this part of the world is impracticable, that it is a grand healthy sport, and opens up many new vistas. In common with many other people, I should also like to appeal for the retention of the old bridle and packhorse tracks, and even for the opening up of new ones, to revive this now neglected pastime.

EDITH BOON

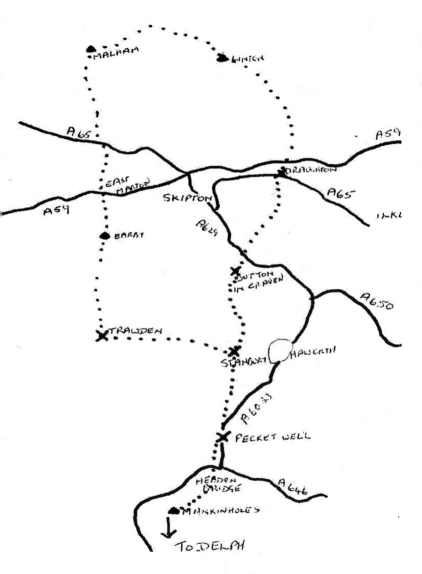

Round Skipton 1950

"Around Skipton."
1950

Edith Boon, Burnedge Riding School, "The Nook," Lydgate, Oldham.
Reg. Lees, Hollings, Oldham.
Ron Mellor, Hollinwood, Oldham.
Margery Walker, Newton Heath, Manchester.

Itinerary.

1) Saturday June 17th, Hollingworth Lake (lunch), Mankinholes Y.H.A

2) Sunday June 18th, "The Packhorse" Wadsworth (lunch), "The Silent Inn" Stanbury.

3) Monday June 19th, "The Herders" Trewden, (lunch) Jerusalem Y.H.A

4) Tuesday June 20th, "Cross Keys", East Marton (lunch) Bell Buck Guest House.

5) Wednesday June 21st, "The Buck" Malham, (lunch) Malham Y.H.A.

6) Thursday June 22nd, Mrs. Bownas, Linton, (lunch) Linton.

7) Friday June 23rd, "Red Lion" Burnsall, (lunch) Draughton Post Office.

8) Saturday June 24th, "Black Horse" Sutton, (lunch) Stanbury.

9) Sunday June 25th, "Robin Hood" Peckett Well, (lunch) Mankinholes Y.H.A.

10) Monday June 26th, Café at Hollingworth Lake. (lunch).

We now feel we can claim this mode of travel as attractive and successful for folks interested in the natural, geographical and historical aspects of our countryside. The height gained by being mounted is of value, a good observation post. As an exercise in careful map reading it is unsurpassed, but a map does not indicate a locked gate, or broken down bridge and unfordable stream.

This year we chose to encircle Skipton. A very wise choice it proved to be, Lancashire and Yorkshire hospitality overwhelming us from beginning to end of our journey. Lunches, evening meals, bed & breakfasts for the 10 days were planned beforehand. One becomes very tired and hungry on a journey of this kind, and we were made happy and comfortable at every resting place, especially at the modernised old inns each lunchtime. The horses too seemed well satisfied for they returned tired, but still sleek.

Variety is the spice of the unconventional holiday, as much as of the conventional one. First we walked, trotted and cantered over familiar moorland and valley (reservoir-filled) tracks. After lunch at Hollingworth Lake we cantered quite long sections of canal towpath, until we left it to climb steeply over a hilly shoulder by way of a packhorse road to our destination, Mankinholes Y.H.A. under Stoodley Pike. The warden, Arthur Archer, was formerly a member of an Oldham climbing group and his wife a member of an Oldham Cycling club.

The next day we travelled by lanes and even woodland ways till we reached the wilder moorland again towards Howarth. On Sunday night we slept not far from Wuthering Heights.

Again on Monday we went over to warmer

countryside round Jerusalem Farm, Y.H.A. Each day we climbed over and on. By Tuesday we left behind the gritstone and enjoyed the green lanes of richer pasturelands south west of Skipton. Then we entered the lanes of grey stonewalls while riding into Malham. The afternoon and evening were spent running in Malham Cove and experiencing the chill of the deep cleft of Goredale Scar.

Much interest was taken in food (Yorkshire pudding) throughout the journey, and there was much food for thought and much humour in our interesting contacts. In the Malham hostel we met a group of boys from a school in Blackburn and a group of children from a co-educational Quaker School. There was no lack of subjects for discussion every day over lunch and at night before retiring. It is perhaps interesting to note that little more than comments on the flora and fauna of the countryside were possible while actually riding. Conversation flourished pleasantly when we were comfortably seated round a fire or inn table. Much helpful information was gleaned from farmers, villagers or other revellers, which helped us on the next stage of our journey.

Thursday was a splendid riding day, for we cantered over grassy moors above Malham, then left them behind as we dropped down to Linton in Wharfedale, where limestone gradually gave way to gritstone. We spent the afternoon browsing over the history of Linton, in its old church.

Friday was the day of lovely Wharfedale villages, Grassington, Hebden, Turnsall for lunch, then Appletreewick and on to the little known village of Draughton for an evening meal, bed and breakfast. This night we took a bus ride into Skipton and spent sometime admiring the old town.

It was Saturday that we completed our circle and returned to Stanbury near Haworth, where we had stayed on the outward journey. Friends from the Oldham district met us here. They had come over to see the Bronte country. We had lunch together at the "Robin Hood" in Peckett Well above Hardcastle Crags. It only remained now for us to find more green lanes and packhorse tracks to lead us back to Mankinholes. From there we retraced our steps to arrive home about five o'clock, June 26th.

EDITH BOON

"Exploring The Local Pennines By Packhorse Roads."
1950

Oldhamers, Joan Travis, Margery Carey, Brian Hough, Fred Dransfield, Charles Armitage and Edith Boon toured, for four September days, interesting and thought-provoking tracks within a fifteen mile radius of our town. We were carried over this rather strenuous route by six willing cobs and ponies. The little black pony was the only one not used to such a journey, but she enjoyed it and was lively and full of mischief to the end of the holiday. All the horses showed delight at the variety of tracks and were inspired by the promise of "pastures new" every lunchtime and evening. Three sacks of food were sent on, but one went astray. To help our mounts we took the very minimum of weight, but as usual the heavy riding macintosh could not be left behind.

Many people from this district will be familiar with our first day's ride, "Lark Hill" moorland tracks near Standedge Cutting and then Wessenden Valley with its two mile canter to the lodge for lunch. (The horses know this track and enjoy it for there is much soft going.) All went well and without incident until the new part of the journey was reached, where we found a gully across an old cart track. With a little encouragement the horses negotiated the cleft, one or two preferring to jump the small stream in the bottom. That night was spent at Holmfirth Youth Hostel.

The next day we made for Marsden down Wessenden Valley. How different from the journey up;

it is remarkable how a scene changes from another viewpoint. Out of Marsden we climbed steeply on to the flat top and then over narrow moorland tracks to Nont Sarah's for lunch. The New Inn, Ripponden was to be our resting place on Sunday night. The afternoon ride passed without remarkable incident for we travelled by old lanes, unfortunately newly macadamed. No day passed without exclamations of delight at the scenic beauty, especially the deep wooded valleys on the leeward side of our hills. There was much comment on the vivid green oases - the smallholdings - contrasting strongly with the extensive stretches of neglected grassland, much of it not in the water catchments areas. Light heartedness seemed the feeling common to all on reaching the New Inn; there was a little stiffness and sleepiness, but none complained of being really tired.

Rainy Monday was the day of excitement. The morning passed uneventfully until we tried to drop down from the moorland plateau into Cragg Village. We were to have lunch at the Hinchcliffe Arms, which we could see down below, and we were hungry as usual. The only way down for us was by a packhorse track, which dropped almost perpendicularly into the village. We dismounted and moved very slowly down in single file. The horses clambered cleverly over the stone slabs, which through years of neglect have slipped into impossible positions. The hazardous descent was worthwhile for none of us had seen Cragg before. The church with the old stone inn behind stood in a pleasant setting of big trees, with a background of bare hillsides. After lunch we set out in a rainstorm, but found a grassy track by Withens Reservoir. At length this track petered out. We knew that ahead we should come upon another piece of the packhorse track, on top, near Stoodley Pike. However, between these two points, we found ourselves in a treacherous bog. Silver, the leader, went down and came out a skewbald. After a very anxious half hour we came upon the promised track and cautiously stepped down to Mankinholes Y.H.A. and found a warm welcome there.

On Tuesday morning we took up the packhorse track almost where we had left it the day before. It led us over a windy shoulder from which we had a magnificent view of the Todmorden district, bathed in sunlight. The canal towpath helped us through the narrow industrialised valley by Walsden, and then we climbed out again and over to the Moorcock, Blackstone Edge Road, where we dined. Horses have an uncanny sense of direction and anticipated the last lap. That afternoon we travelled fast over a moorland cart track, then down to Hollingworth Lake. About Rakewood we used much persuasion and example, by wading, to bring all the horses through a deep, rushing stream, where there had once been a bridge. The rest of the journey was long and slow by Ogden and Captain's Edge. However, we finished strongly over Highmoor to reach home, behind familiar Wharmton in daylight.

EDITH BOON

"Round The Peak."
1951

Having finished lunch at Mr. Mason's Cottage "Brushes Clough" on Sunday July 1st, we faced the ride home, but before saddling up for the last time we lounged in sunshine recapturing some of the incidents of our journey. Since the daily rides have been varied we found it hard to say which we most appreciated, so we relived the whole journey by reading our diary.

"Wakes" Saturday June 23 1951.

Set out from Wade Hill about ten o'clock. First canter enjoyed over Lark Hill as mist cleared in "Ammon Wrigley's" Castleshaw Valley. Later mystery introduced by trek over open moor to avoid busy Standedge Cutting. Elevenses at 'Hare and Hounds' Marsden. Long canter through lower Wessendon Valley to Wessendon Lodge, Mrs. Skyes had had lunch all ready. Fast riding followed, but missed equestrian entertainment at Harden Moss Sheep Dog Trials. Mr. and Mrs. O'Grady entertained us at Wood Cottage Youth Hostel.

Sunday June 24 1951
.

Cantered over half-built embankment of resorvoir on site of former Holmebridge Lodge. Climbed to Holme, then proceeded below Holme Moss TV mast.

Then waited a few moments to admire a charming wooded valley, zigzagged steeply to Cook's Study and cantered on to Snittlegate Café. Continued via Flouch-Langsett-Midhope-Bolsterstones then dropped down to Ewden Waterworks and village Y.H.A. Spent evening in enlightening and amusing conversation.

Monday June 25 1951.

Rest day for the horses, rushed to Billy Green at Langsett – No lunch – rushed to Sheffield – good lunch. Spent evening cleaning tack.

Tuesday June 26 1951.

Pleasant morning ride despite rain. Impressed by fairy story atmosphere around Wigtwizzle and Agden Lodge. Excellent lunch provided by Mrs. Willis, Strines Inn. Regulars tried to sell us sheep dog pup or take a horse in part ex. Landlord wanted Silver for rounding up the sheep. Passed by Lady Bower Reservoir, crossed Yorkshire Bridge and on through lovely lanes to Pindale and Castleton.

Wednesday June 27 1951.

Castleton to Edale via Brough and Shatton, along narrow ways to attractive modernised Coaching Inn, "The Rising Sun" at Hope. Again spent much time over excellent cuisine and conversation. Momentary anxiety on thinking horses gone, found in the long grass. More lanes and soft going, then "Hope Cross" on the shoulder of Win Hall – manoeuvred horses through Jagger's Clough to reach Edale Y.H.A.

Thursday June 28 1951.

Rest Day for the horses. We walked to foot of Jacob's Ladder reconnoitering for bridle tracks. Whilst cleaning tack at Hostel exchanged notes with walkers, cyclist and school party leaders.

Friday June 29 1951.

Increased romance and thrill of journey by using the ancient cart track Edale to Tideswell. At Mam Nick refreshing breezes cooled us as we reined in to marvel at the contrast in scenery. Left cart track, dismounted and then led horses down to Winnate pass. Afternoon spent visiting caverns at Castleton.

Saturday June 30 1951.

Bad luck today - long duties at Hostel delayed our progress up Pindale to a rider's paradise – Dirtlow Rake. Reached old bridle track, Perryfoot to Hayfield, via Heych Clough. Between South Head and Mount Famine, thrilled with riding at a height of 1700ft. Delightful meal at Tunsted House, more bad luck – Dolly found to have loose shoes; then climbed over Lantern Pike to Howarth. Found a good Samaritan in Mr. Cox – blacksmith-cum-farmer. After supper at Anderton House, Rowarth, met friends at the "Little Mill Inn" situated at the end of a motor road cul de sac.

Sunday July 1 1951.

Hilly ride in great heat via Charlesworth, Broadbottom, Mottram and beautiful lane near Hollingworth Hall to late lunch at Brushes Clough.

Dolly, owned and ridden by Mrs.Mary Lees, Punch, owned by Mrs Boon and ridden by Miss Hillary Butterworth, Silver owned and ridden by Mrs. Boon, carried us safely home, completing an almost perfect circle using only a few miles of main road.

EDITH BOON

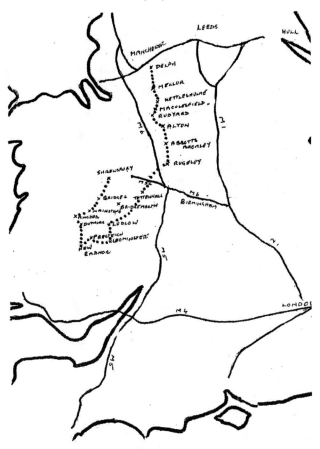

Saddleworth To Severn Country 1952

"From Saddleworth To The Severn Country."
(A proposed Long Journey)
1952

Aug 9…Hattersley, Mottram Rowarth Mellor (Cheshire) 16 miles

Aug 10…Windgather YHA Windgather Kettleshulme (Cheshire) 8 miles

Aug 11…Windgather YHA Oakenclough YHA (Macclesfield) 8 miles

Aug 12…New Inn (Winkle) Hotel Rudyard (Staffs) 10 miles

Aug 13…Rudyard Village P.O., Sharpcliffe YHA Staffs 8 miles

Aug 14 …Shrewsbury Hotel Alton Towers Staffs 9 miles

Aug 15…Red Lion Inn Uttoxeter Abbots Bromley 14 miles

Aug 16…Wandon YHA (Rugeley) 9 miles

Aug 17   Inn-Inn Tettenhall Staffs 15 miles

Aug 18   Inn-Fosters Arms Bridgenorth 10 miles

Aug 19   Inn Wilderhope YHA (Wenlock) 12 miles

Aug 20   Star and Garter and Ludlow YHA 14 miles

Aug 21   Stone House Kingsland Leominster 12 miles

Aug 22 Barley Mow Presteigne, Farington Farm (Knighton) 14 miles

Aug 23   The Eagle New Radnor, Forest Inn (Radnor) 13 miles

Aug 24   The Severn Arms The Warfe Llandewi 10 miles

Aug 25   Inn, Inn Duthlas Radnor 10 miles
Aug 26   The Anchor Inn Clun Forest Radnor 6 miles
Aug 27   The Reilth Mainstone (A farm- friends) 6
            miles
Aug 28   The Three Horse Shoes and Bridges YHA
                (Longmynd) 16 miles
Aug 29   Shrewsbury (Salop) Aunties
Aug 30   Entrain for home Shrewsbury Station.

On this journey Edith rode a 13-year-old grey mare
'Silver' and her friend Miss Mary Lees 'Dolly' a bay 6
years old hunter. Parcels of clothing were posted on at
three-day intervals (those were the days when you
could rely on your parcels being delivered overnight.)

"Yorkshire Dales And The North Yorkshire Moors"
1957

Date	Journey	Distance.
4th Aug	To Cragg Vale via Hollingworth Lake	18m
5th Aug	Howarth via Wainstalls and Oxenhope	13m
6th Aug	Burleywoodhead via Moorland Road	15m
7th Aug	Dacre Banks via Moor Track and Blubberhouses	12m
8th Aug	Ellingstring via Fountaines Abbey and Masham	24m
9th Aug	Carlton Miniott near Thirsk	10m
10th Aug	Sutton Bank Agric Show-	
11th Aug	Rode with friends round Carlton	5m
12th Aug	Fangdale Beck Bilsdale	12m
15th Aug	Westerdale via Chopgate	?
14th Aug	Farndale YH at Church House	7m
15th Aug	Rest Day	
16th Aug	Hunt House Y.H.A	10m
17th Aug	Lockton Y.H.A	20m
18th Aug	Kirby Moorside	?
19th Aug	Malton	?
20th Aug	York	15m
21st Aug	York	5m
22nd Aug	Spoffath	10m
23rd Aug	Harrogate	13m
24th Aug	Howarth	10m
25th Aug	Mankinholes via Heptonstall	10m
26th Aug	Home via Walsden and Hollingworth Lake	18m

(The information sheet on this ride was damaged and some information was illegible).

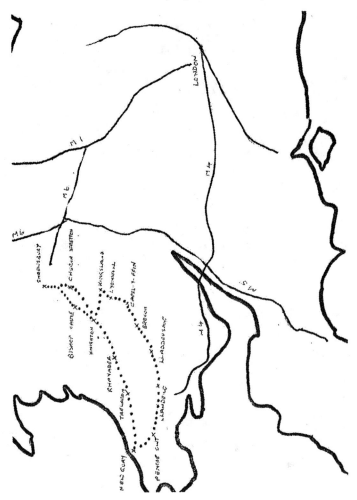

Shrewsbury Circle 1961

"Shrewsbury Circle."
1961

Mon. Aug 14
Stayed: Shrewsbury
Accommodation: Friend
Notes: Box to start, rest day.

Tue. Aug 15
Stayed: Bishop's Gate
Accommodation: Guest house
Notes: Coffee at Leebot Wood, Tea at Gliding Club Longmynd

Wed. Aug 16
Stayed: Knighton
Accommodation: Farm
Notes: Lunch, sandwiches White Horse, Clun

Thu. Aug 17
Stayed: Rhayader
Accommodation: Trekking Centre
Notes: Lunch, sandwiches Seven Arms Hotel Penybont

Fri. Aug 18
Stayed: Tregaron
Accommodation: Railway Inn
Notes: Lunch Pontrhyd y Groes nr Devils Bridge, Blacksmith

Sat. Aug 19
Stayed: Llanarth,
Accommodation: Friend
Notes: Lunch Talsarn Nr Newquay

Sun. Aug 20
REST DAY

Mon. Aug 21
Stayed: Pentre Cwrt.
Accommodation: Youth Hostel
Notes: Lunch (free) Talgareg, Llandyssul. Blacksmith
Pont Shaen

Tue. Aug 22
Stayed: Salem Llandeilo
Accommodation: Friend
Notes: Pancakes Brechfa

Wed. Aug 23
Stayed: Llandeusant
Accommodation: Youth Hostel
Notes: Lunch, sandwiches Llandgadog

Thu. Aug 24
Stayed: Tyn-y-Caeau
Accommodation: Youth Hostel
Notes: Lunch Trecastle. Blacksmith Senny Bridge

Fri. Aug 25
Rest Day. Visited CRICKHOWELL by bus 'Bunty'
slight accident

Sat. Aug 26
Stayed: Capel-y-Ffin
Accommodation: Youth Hostel
Notes: Sandwiches at foot of 'The Grid' went over the
mountain

Sun. Aug 27
Stayed: Lyonshall
Accommodation: Youth Hostel
Notes: Lunch at Hay

Mon. Aug 28
Stayed: Kingsland
Accommodation: Friend
Notes: Lunch Baron's Cross

Tue. Aug 29
Stayed: Knighton
Accommodation: Farm
Notes: Lunch Lingen

Wed. Aug 30
Stayed: Church Stretton
Accommodation: Friend
Notes: Lunch Kangaroo Aston on Club

Thu. Aug 31
Stayed: Shrewsbury
Accommodation: Friend
Notes: Lunch Leebotswood

Edith's mount on this journey was 'Bunty', a grey mare that she had when I first met her in 1956.

When looking at Edith's route it must be remembered that in 1961 there was far less traffic than today, and most freight went by rail rather than by road. This means that the 'A' roads were quieter than the present 'B' roads.

Edith's maps of the first 3 days and the last 2 days

are in my possession so the given route is accurate on these days, although it is probable that she made diversions to view churches and other monuments. On other days I have given the most probable route using the information about lunch stops etc.

August 15
A49 to Leebotwood, then Long Mynd to A489 and on to Bishops Castle

August 16
A488 to Clun and Knighton Farm at Farrington to S.E.

August 17
A 488 to Penybont then A44 to Rhayader.

August 18
A44 to B 4343 to Devils Bridge then on to Pontrhyd Y Groes and Tregaron.

August 19
B4342 via Llangeitho to Talsan then B4342 via Ystrad Aeron and Dihewid to
Llanarth

August 20
A487 to Synod Inn, then B4338 to Talgarreg, B 4459 to Pont Saen and on to B4336 and A486 to Pentre Cwrt
August 21 REST DAY

August 22
White roads to B4459 and Pencader, white roads to Gwyddgrug then A485 to New Inn. The white road to Brechfa and the B 4310 to A 40 to Llandeilo.

August 23

A40 to A4069 Llangadog. The A4069 to white road to Twyn Llanan and Llanddeusant Youth Hostel.

August 24

White road via Talsarn to Trecastle and A40 to Senny Bridge. Continuing on A40 to Brecon and Youth Hostel.

August 25

Due to slight injury to Bunty, a rest day. Edith took bus into Crickhowell.

August 26

A470 to A479 Talgarth, then white roads past hospital and Sychnant Farm to R.U.P.P. over mountain and past Grwyne Fawr reservoir to woods, then left onto bridleway to Capel Y Ffin Youth hostel.

August 27

White road through Gospel Pass to Hay On Wye then B4350 to A438 through
Whitney to A4111, then white roads to Lyonshall.

August 28

White roads to A4362 Shobden, then white roads to Kingsland.

August 29

A4110 to Lucton then white roads to Lingen and Knighton.

August 30

A4113 and B4367 to Aston On Clun, then white roads

to A489 via Hederley.
B4370 to Marshbrook then white road to Little Stretton
and B4370 to Church Stretton.

August 31
A49 to Shrewsbury with lunch at Leebotwood.

"Lancashire and Yorkshire."
1964
By Jean.

Delph to Mankinholes Youth Hostel. Mary Archer, the Warden was an old friend of Edith's. Put horses in a field nearby. Went by way of Rakewood and valley pack horse road over to Lumbutts.

From Mankinholes, either by way of Heptenstall or Peckett Well, to Barley Youth Hostel. We went into Nelson for a Chinese meal, the first I had had. It was very cheap with pineapple fritters for afters. In Nelson we met up with my parents who were trying to find us, then we returned to the Youth Hostel. Whilst we had been away there had been a cloudburst and thunder storm and Cloud, my pony, had jumped out of the field over the railings in his fright, into a cabbage patch. He tried to jump back again, but the soft ground did not give him the chance of a clean take off and he must have got his back legs down between the horizontal railings and he had grazed the hair off his cannon bones. Edith, in a panic, " Don't get the vet, he'll send us home," put some Acriflavine on (she always carried some medication in her saddlebags) and it healed up in a few days.

We helped clear out a cottage that was flooded; the water had run right through it. There was a lot of silt that we had to shovel out, and move carpets etc. The householders were not insured.

I think we then went through Downham to Slaidburn and from there via Tosside and the Donkey Sanctuary to Stainforth. We had lunch at a pub in

Giggleswick, putting the horses in a field as we usually did if we could at lunchtime. On the way back to the field we met an old man walking, who, with hindsight, must have had a gill or two. We were on a path next to a stream and there were some cottages nearby. The man asked if I was Edith's daughter. No. Was she married? No. Well if she was interested he had a lovely cottage over there. Was it a proposal?

We went on to stay at Stainforth YHA (I think it had a paddock in front of it or that may have been Slaidburn.)

From Stainforth we went over the tops to Kettlewell YHA and from there via Elnsey Crag (horses in field and lunch at pub) over the tops again via Malham Tarn down to Settle but we went through and stayed B&B in village. It was COLD; no heating in August. We put riding macs over bannisters to dry (at this time riding macs were rubberised fawn cotton and very hard to dry). The horses were put in a field surrounding a Catholic church with hardly any fencing or wall, but they did not escape (too hungry). This was a rare event in that accommodation had not been prearranged for the horses or us. Same thing at Gisburn, where we were 'put up' in a cottage on Main Street and had our meals at hotel. It may have been from here that we stayed at Earby YHA- very new and 'posh'. Sprung interior mattresses and carpets, and rooms for 4 or so, not large dormitories.

We then came back via Mankinholes. We had several ways of getting to and from Mankinholes and I cannot remember which was used on which occasion. We sometimes used Cragg Vale.

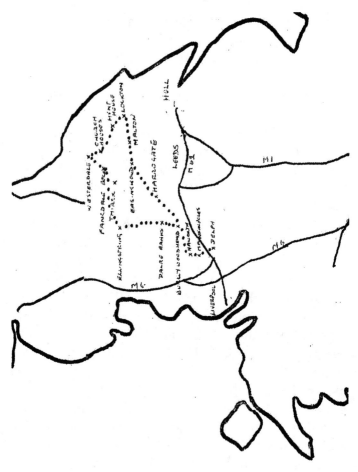

North Yorkshire To East Coast 1964

"North Yorkshire Journey To East Coast."
1964

August

Monday 8	Mankinholes Y.H.A
Tuesday 9	Haworth Y.H.A
Wednesday 10	Burleywoodhead Y.H.A
Friday 12	Ellingstring Y.H.A
Sat/Sun 13/14	Thirsk
Monday 15	Fangdale Beck
Tuesday 16	Westerdale Y.H.A
Wed/Thur 17/18	Church House
Friday 19	Hunt House Y.H.A
Saturday 20	Lockton Y.H.A
Sunday 21	Malton Y.H.A
Mon/Tue 22/23	Easingwold
Wednesday 24	Harrogate YMCA
Thursday 25	Burley Woodhead
Friday 26	Haworth Y.H.A
Saturday 27	Mankinholes Y.H.A
Sunday 28	Home

Aug 8 and 9

As previous routes to Haworth

Aug 10

A 6033 to Junction with A629, straight across to minor road over Harden Moor to Harden and B6429 to

A650. Right, then left past railway station to Eldwick. At 'Y' junction left to pub then right and lanes towards Menston and Burley Woodhead.

Aug 11

Lane past Cow And Calf rocks to Ilkley. Left after station and straight across A65 by church and after crossing river, right on lane to Askwith. Left past chapel and at cross roads left to Blubberhouses. Right on A59 and left into lane past Hardisty Hill, 2nd lane right passing Carrlow Ridge Plantation, left and keeping due north, lanes to B6451 and YHA at Dacre Bank.

Aug 12

B6451 to 36165 at Summer Bridge, then left to Wilsill. Right across B6265 into lane over Pateley Moor. At junction right into unfenced road and on to Laverton, Kirkby Malzeard and Grewelthorpe bearing left and passing south of Nutwith and Roomer Common, then west of Swinton Park to Healey; then right to YHA at Ellingstrings.

Aug 13

Lanes to Fearby and Masham, then A6108 to B6267 to Mowbray Hill; then right to West Tanfield and A6108. Left and immediate left on lane to Wath; then bear left to Middleton Quernhow. Right to A1 and across onto bridleway to Howe and B6267. Right to A61, left through Skipton On Swale. Right onto bridleway to Waters House and A167. Left then right onto bridleway past Coronation Whin, to A61 to Carlton Miniott.

Aug 14. REST DAY.

Aug 15

Left into lane at Carlton House, then right into bridleway passing Carr Plantation, Woodhill Grange, Underwood Plantation to B 1448. Bridleway crossing over river to South Kilvington and A19. Lane past Manor House, and bridleway past Hag House to Felixkirk. Left past church then right for Boltby. Up steep hill and over hilltop and down to Hawnby. Right up steep hill, down and across river then left onto bridleway through Banniscue Woods, Ewe Cote, Helm House to YHA at Fangdale Beck.

Aug 16

Left on 91257 then right into bridleway to Bonfield Ghyll, left on lane to Cockayne and on to Westerby YHA.

Aug 17 and 18

Church House YHA.

Aug 19

It is not apparent how Edith planned this route as her maps were very small scale and do not give enough information. The best I can work out is:-

South on lanes to Hutton Le Hole, then east to Lastingham, Low Askew, Cropton, Cawthorne; then north on tracks and bridleways to Stape and through Cropton Forest to YHA Whelldale Lodge (Hunt House).

Aug 20

Bridleway over Simon Howe Rigg to Wardle Rigg and following Newton Dale to Lockton YHA.

Aug 21

Lane to A169, then right to Inn and left into lane to Thornton Dale. Cross A170 and past church following lane to bridleway at Flat Top House. Right onto bridleway to Wray House and Prospect House Farm across A169 into lane to Kirkby Misperton; then left to Great Haston. Left to Ryton, cross the river and, after Eden House, bridleways on right to B1257. Across and on to A64 and YHA at Malton.

Aug 22

Lane to Coneysthorpe, left, passing Castle Howard on left, then right to Bulmer and Sheriff Hutton, Marton In The Forest and B1363 at Stillington. At church straight on into lane for Easingwold.

Aug 23 REST DAY

Aug 24

Crossing A19 lane towards Raskelf, then first left at The Green, crossing railway to Tholthorpe and keeping west on to Myton On Swale. Right onto bridleway to Clott House Farm, then lane to cross A1 near campsite and on to Miniskip.

South on A6055, then lane and bridleway to Arkendale and Flaxby to A59. Right and left to Goldsborough, then bridleway passing Birkham Wood and Plompton Hall. Cross A661 into lane to Follifoot.

NOTE: This area is now much altered by new roads, so consult new map before trying to follow Edith's route.

Aug 25

Lanes to Kirkby Overblow and south to Netherby. Bridleway west along River Wharfe to A61. Left to A659 then right and bridleway on left through North Park to Weardley.

Lane to Eccup, then right past Blackhill Farm; right again on bridleway on left past Wood Top Farm to Bramhope. Left onto A660 then right to Old Bramhope. Cross A658 and by way of The Chevin cross railway and straight across the A road to Menston and Burley Wood Head.

Aug 26, 27 and 28 as route out.

To Robin Hood's Bay, Yorkshire Coast
1964

By Jean. Riders: Edith on "Ted", Jean on "Scout".

Set off from Delph to Mankinholes YHA where there was a new warden and wife who had re-decorated the hostel with pale green emulsion walls and chestnut doors. It looked very smart. Went from there to Haworth via Peckett Well. We looked around the Bronte Parsonage and stayed at YHA. There was a field very near. Haworth was not a tourist place then as it is now, just quaint.

Next stop, Burley in Warfedale YHA. Horses quite a hike away up a hill. Cleaned tack I remember. We then went via Blubberhouses and Brimham Rocks to Dacre Bank YHA. It was an old school which had been converted.

From there we went to Fountains Abbey, put the horses in a field and looked around. Again it was not touristy. A long ride from there on wide verges of main road to Carlton Miniott near Thirsk to stay with friends who had a place for horses at the back of the cottage. We stayed a day or two and went on bus trip, to Ripon I think it was.

From Carlton Miniott we trudged up Sutton Bank on our way to Helmsley via Rievaulx Abbey where we had a look around. We stayed with relatives of friends in Thirsk in a farm at Helmsley. It was COLD - no heating).

From there we made our way over Fylingdales moor to YHA at Robin Hoods Bay where we shared a room with two girls who came in late and drunk. One was sick. They got into trouble with the warden. They had been to a party on the beach and lots of bottles were left around. We rode the horses on the beach and paddled them in the sea.

Ted always recognised the YHA sign and Scout would pull up if we said, "It's just over there." I think we came back through Thornton-le-Dale and probably stayed at Malham We called in and looked around Castle Howard. We were allowed to put our horses in the stables (pre-Flamingo Land).

From there we went to York and YHA. Very busy. We rode right through centre. Quite a frightening experience even given that the traffic of those days was nothing like as bad as it is today. We met some girls from New Zealand, and then we moved on and stayed at Pannal near Harrogate and put the horses in a field on a nearby farm which has now been built on. (Near the old Cattle Market). I think we looked round Harewood House. I cannot remember how we got back to Mankinholes and then home again.

At one point we rode along an old Roman Road, I think it may have been on the North Yorks. Moors. There was a notice forbidding one to ride horses on the Roman Road, which was very rough and stony - who would want to? I also think it was on this journey we stayed in the middle of a forest in a YHA which was just a little cottage with no amenities. The bathroom was in an outhouse, no hot water, and it was only open in summer. Nothing to do but read and go to bed early.

We always rode where possible on what are now bridlepaths, but then were just lanes and tracks not designated as now. Calls of nature were answered behind a wall or hedge and lunch was sometimes nonexistent. We would stop at a 'Sunblest' van and buy a pie or two or maybe we would come across a shop; only occasionally did we find a pub and not many catered in those days. We did have the odd glass of sherry.

One time I remember the horses shared a field with some campers. The horses were fascinated by their tent and wouldn't keep away. The occupants were terrified. We told them the horses were just being nosey and looking for tit bits, but they were still afraid. Scout was always bad to catch at home, but on a trek he was amenable to being in a strange field and frightened of being left behind.

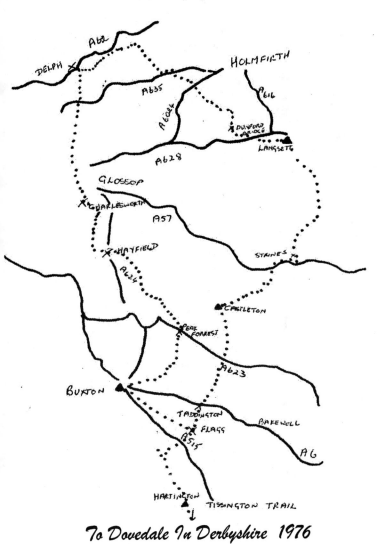

To Dovedale In Derbyshire 1976

Barbara Haigh

"To Dovedale in Derbyshire."
1976

Friday	Lunch 'Stanhope Arms Dunford Bridge	Grazing .50p
June 18	Dinner Inn Langsett	Grazing .50p
	B&B YHA .93p and £2.91	
Saturday	Lunch 'The Strines Inn'	Grazing .50p
June 19	Dinner Restaurant Castleton	
	B&B YHA Castleton £4.20p and £1.40p	Grazing .50p
Sunday	Lunch 'The Waterloo' Taddington	Grazing .50p
June 20	Dinner 'The Royal Oak'	
	B&B Flagg	Grazing .50p
Monday	Lunch on Trail	Grazing .50p
June 21	Dinner Izaak Walton Hotel	
	B&B Dovedale	Grazing .50p
Tuesday	Lunch 11am	
June 22	Dinner Izaak Walton Hotel	Grazing .50p
Rest Day	B&B Dovedale Mon and Tue £12.45	
Wednesday	Lunch on Trail	
June 23	Dinner 'Old Devonshire Arms'	
	B&B Hartington	Grazing .50p
Thursday	Lunch 'Royal Oak' Flagg	Grazing .50p
June 24	Dinner Restaurant Buxton	
	B&B YHA Buxton £4.80 and £1.60	Grazing .50p
Friday	Lunch 'Devonshire Arms' Peak Forest	Grazing .50p
June 25	Dinner Huntsman Hayfield	
	B&B The George Hayfield	Grazing .50p
Saturday	Lunch 'Hunters Arms' Charlesworth	Grazing .50p
June 26	Dinner Home	Hunt Kennels
	B&B Home	

FRIDAY June 18

Crinkle Corner Cottage, left on A62 then first left

past Knarr Cottages and at top of hill left into Delph village. Through village over bridge then right on lane to A62. Straight across onto old road up to Harrop Edge. Left at top of hill and along old road to rejoin A62.

Right, then first left on lane running parallel with A62 behind the 'Horse and Jockey'. This becomes a track and rejoins A62 at Standedge. Cross A62 into car park and take bridleway over top of cutting to gate leading to grassy track with reservoir on left.

At next road right turn down hill towards Marsden then right again into Wessenden Valley, now a definitive bridleway due in parts to Edith's efforts. This leads to A635 Isle Of Skye Road. Left onto road, then after about 1 mile bridleway on right leads down past old farms to lane leading to Holmbridge.

Right onto A6024 past 'The Fleece' (good food) then, at bends where hill starts, left onto tracks past Ramsden Reservoir, following Ramsden Road and white roads to Dunford Bridge, and lunch.

Windle Edge to bridleway past Upper Windleden Reservoir and on to A628. Left then left onto bridleway Snow Road. When it rejoins A628, left, then right into Swinden Lane to A616 and Langsett Youth Hostel.

SATURDAY June 19

Pass Langsett Reservoir on road to Midhope, Arden Bridge and Strines for lunch.

When lane reaches A57, right to A6013, left, then right over Yorkshire Bridge, then left and follow lanes to Hope. Cross A625 and follow lanes to Castleton Youth Hostel.

SUNDAY June 20

Lanes skirting quarry in Pin Dale, then right towards Bradwell Moor, passing 'The Holmes' and the Batham Gate Roman Road to A623. Cross road into lane to Wheston, then lane to Monksdale House and track to Millersdale.

B6049 towards Taddington and bridleway by 'The Waterloo' to A6 Cross A6 onto lanes to High Peak Trail and Royal Oak.

MONDAY June 21

High Peak and Tissington Trail to Fenny Bently, then lanes to Ilam and 'Izaac Walton Hotel'.

TUESDAY June 22
REST DAY.

WEDNESDAY June 23

Tissington Trail to Hartington.

THURSDAY June 24

Leave Hartington by lane past Moat Hall to Pilsbury and on to High Peak Trail to 'Royal Oak' for lunch.

Lanes and track to youth hostel at Buxton.

FRIDAY June 25

Harper Hill to A515 at Heathfield Nook. Straight across main road to lane leading to Cowdale, turning right to King Sterndale and A6. Right, then left into bridleway through Wooldale and on to Lowfoot Farm. At Daisymere Farm, right into bridleway and lanes to Hardybarn, then bridleway to Tunstead and lanes to Peak Forrest and lunch.

Perry Dale leads to B6061, left, then immediate right past Rushop Hall to go straight across A625 onto bridleway past Mount Famine to Hayfield.

SATURDAY June 26

NOTE - due to new bridleways being opened since this ride, and Edith using private land for part of the route, I have altered this days route slightly, as Edith would have done.

Sett Valley Trail to Station Road, then right and right again behind the houses onto bridleway which leads over Lantern Pike and Matley Moor to Monks Road. Left onto Monks Road. Part way down there is a bridleway on the left which saves a very steep slippery part of Monks Road, and rejoins it near Charlesworth.

Due to barriers, it is now necessary to follow main road to Mottram and then the A601B past the 'Roe Cross'. Next right up cobbled lane and left through farmyard onto track behind new estate and on to Brushes Country Park.

Pass Brushes Reservoir, then left to Sun Hill. Right up hill, to Mooredge Road and Abraham's Chair to

Greenfield, bridleway to Uppermill and Delph Donkey bridleway back to Crinkle Corner Cottage.

A Brief Account

"Comparisons are odious" but, now that we have two holiday rides accomplished, comparison is difficult to avoid. It was declared that the first ride of seven days was better than the one of nine days, mainly because the weather was cold and damp. The second ride which it is now my pleasure to comment upon, took place in that period of remarkably hot sunny weather last summer. Day after day we baked; as you all know one is very exposed on horseback. Also we could not ask for a trot, and certainly not a canter, even when conditions underfoot were favourable. The exception was the first day, the day of the marathon, when much of the day was cold, windy and wet, with road work necessary towards the end of the day. Both journeys were designed from home outwards; this meant riding through millstone-grit scenery to the warm limestone type, so both were equally rewarding from a scenic point of view. Trekking has so many other delights, however, so it is wise to record the highlights through a day-by-day commentary.

The day of the marathon ride was very pleasantly typical of our local beauty. Tracks led us first across peaty moorland then into and through Pennine valleys. Because the latter contain reservoirs, the rights of way are controlled by the Water Authority. It would appear that the Authority is anti-bridleway, although declaring in a publication that it is pro-all sporting activities. However, clever and artistic flowery landscaping gave us great joy visually, especially the banks of rhododendrons, with scents of mixed woodland dominated by heavy hawthorn scent. For many miles we rode through a miniature Lakeland, with waterfalls and rushing streams to be crossed at the bottom of deep gorges. This area could be a rider's paradise if the Water Authority's restrictions on the use of sandy side tracks were relaxed. Deceivingly long road stretches resulted in our having lunch at 4 p.m. in the Stanhope Arms, Dunford Bridge. We had called there previously by car and reckoned on a late lunch at 2 p.m. The family running the establishment was extremely hospitable, for we arrived wind-blown and very wet at a most inconvenient time. Naturally, we found the meal delicious, and with comforting drinks, we did not face the last lap of six to eight miles until 6 p.m. Our destination was a Youth Hostel at Langsett, a place of very simple clean accommodation, "no meals provided." There was plenty of grass for the horses. So we look ourselves off to the "Pack Horse" across the road and ate and drank ourselves comfortable.

The next day, we took to roads through "Pennine Lakeland" and very beautiful it was; more hawthorn scent and rhododendron displays. Our prearranged luncheon spot was at the "Strines Inn" roughly half way on our route to Castleton. The horses found the shorter rich grazing a delight and a contrast to the previous night's long heavy grass. It was our policy to give them two hours for lunch every day, so we accordingly wined and dined, giggled and gossiped for two hours every day at lunch-time - these two hours seemed to surpass our evenings sometimes. The afternoon trek will be well known, I suppose, for it took us down the Glossop-Sheffield Road to Ladybower Reservoir. Then, following the hillside contour through narrow lanes, edged with a great variety of wild flowers missing in Saddleworth, we reached Hope. My friend, Jack Peake, introduced the horses to yet another rich grazing and took us and our tack etc. by car to Castleton Youth Hostel. Our evening in Castleton was made more pleasurable by the arrival of Irene's visitors. We found the Hostels quite adequate, and breakfasted quite pleasantly at all three hostels that we visited.

The hot weather had started the second day, and on the third day we entered the 'limestone oven' and the land of slippery roads. On our morning phase, we grew weary of old lanes recently Macadamed, large lorries collecting milk in churns and sand or limestone quarries. At Wheston we found a bridleway bounded by high grey walls and pleasantly overgrown. This track dropped us into Millers Dale. At this point we had no previous arrangement but quite quickly found a kindly smallholder who offered grazing, and we lunched in the local. This day we were making for Diana's near Flagg. Now, Diana's needs some explanation. Barbara and I had weeks previously toured the Flag - Monyash area for a third night's resting place, and were unlucky until we were directed to the "Royal Oak" near the Buxton - Ashbourne Railway. This could possibly be what we were looking for, as the disused railway had been converted into the Tissington Trail suitable for riders. The outward appearance of the inn was off-putting, but we bravely knocked. We had found the ideal spot! Diana was the licensee. A smell of homemade bread assailed our nostrils, and on stepping inside we saw dozens of dinner rolls. In no time, we were drinking coffee, and reading a 6-inch to the mile map displayed on the dining room wall. Diana had ridden ponies since she was two, and had many horses and ponies grazing down the lane; her own mount at the time being an attractive Welsh Cob. Still more interesting to us at that moment was that she provided an evening meal, bed and breakfast, and it would be possible for us to stay at the Royal Oak on our third night, and we were to discover that the food was "Cordon Bleu" standard.

Now back to our journey - we climbed out of Millers Dale towards Taddington, and soon on entering the bridleway by the "Waterloo" we met Diana on her Welsh Cob, accompanied by two fellow-riders who had come up the trail to the Royal Oak. One rode a black, recently cut stallion, the other a very heavy Palomino. This, plus two dogs, was our escort, to guide us by lanes and tracks to Diana's place The fellows were to ride, later, back down the Trail to their horsebox and thus return home to the Potteries. That evening Barbara's husband found us enjoying an exotic meal, and of course joined us.

The next morning we actually rode on to the old railway track. At first it was nastily stony, like our own Delph Donkey Trail, but at Parsley Hey it had been suitably surfaced. We rode, free from traffic, along embankments and through cuttings, through mile after mile of glorious panoramas of the rich Derbyshire countryside. The farmers were certainly "making hay while the sun shone". Noise of tractors and farm machinery was all that disturbed the peace. In places, the trail was edged with suitable bushes, and again wild flowers; Campion, Ragged Robin vetches and so on in profusion. We were to leave the trail about 5pm. to make for the "Izaac Walton" Hotel in Dovedale. In the meantime we wanted lunch, and the horses their grazing.

We ventured off the track at a suitable point, usually where a station had been, and found the "New Inn" on the main Buxton - Ashbourne Road. New managers had arrived that morning, but we were made more than welcome, as the landlady had done much riding. Our lunch extended to afternoon tea.

Eventually we returned to the trail, and at a suitable "station" we left it to follow the road to the "Izaac Walton", where Vera was waiting anxiously, with a welcome change of clothing. Here the horses ate too richly, and had a day of rest.

The heat was fierce and flies were a nuisance, but the stay was pleasant. On our day of rest we crossed the Dove by stepping stones, visited the stately home at Ilam and dined in Ashbourne. All this by the fifth day!

As the sixth night was to be spent at Hartington, we decided to use the trail again. Hartington is a most attractive village and some day we must go again for a cream tea in the Saddleroom. "Ye Olde Devonshire Arms", where we lodged, over looked a village green and duckpond, and we found no difficulty in discovering a farmer who took an interest in our travels, and his grazing was again lush.

On the seventh day, we were to make for Buxton, so what more suitable than a lunch break at Diana's? This time we decided not to use the Trail, but an old track typically following a steep-sided valley bottom. We came across a gate and - surprise, surprise - who should be opening it for us but Diana. This time she had come to meet us on a thickset Apaloosa. At this point, we were surrounded by grassy round-topped hills and as we rode out of the narrow valley, guided by Diana, we enjoyed much horsey talk. Diana took us back on the Trail for a short distance, and so back to the "Royal Oak" and a Cordon Bleu lunch. Diana is certainly a "Woman of many parts" There was embroidery to be admired, and each night she presided over the locals and their pints, smoking a clay pipe. Our afternoon's journey to Buxton was uneventful, except for the, to me, unusual-looking "Axe Edge" which was another of the endless memory nudges received daily. We came across a signposted bridleway, which led us into "Arizona" for it petered out in a vast area of worked out quarry. We did eventually find a way out, and slid slowly by road to a good field, and a short distance away was the Buxton Youth Hostel. We were not impressed by Buxton.

Our aim was to return via the "other side" of the Kinder Scout mass, so we chose to stay in Hayfield on the eighth night. Lunch was possible at Peak Forest. Diana and I, on studying the map, had decided that to move on via Cow Dale and Wood Dale. It may be longer, but it would avoid the ugly quarrying areas around Peak Dale. Alas, this did not work out as planned. Around King Sterndale, the scenic beauty was rarely appreciated, but unfortunately we were forced to use the A5 for quite a distance at a point where it runs through a steep-sided, wooded gorge. We escaped from this situation up a very steep, very slippery farm lane to find ourselves in a field with a very dangerous looking bull. Again we escaped to find ourselves in a former "lane" now the main artery to an I.C.I. cement works- biggest and busiest in the world! We did eventually reach the quiet backwater of Peak Forest and spend two hours pleasantly, whilst our faithful friends and fellow sufferers grazed.

The afternoon journey - all tracks on the edge of Kinder Scout via Perrifoot, Royal Clough and Mount Famine - finished in Hayfield. Here again we found folks helpful and interested in our venture.

On the ninth day, we were well into Millstone Grit country again, the scenery not so rich. Up and over we went into the cul-de-sac village of Rowarth, famous for the "Old Mill Inn", now a restaurant of repute. Next tracks up and over again to lunch near the North East Cheshire Drag Hunt kennels at Charlesworth. The horses were delighted - variety is the spice of life, and a corn feed, indoors, was welcome change from the varied grasses they had been fed day after day. The Hunt really did us well. From Woodseats it was easy, via the footbridge over the river Ethrow, and via Broadbottom Woods, to reach Mottram. We looked for Mrs White at Hollingworth Hall Farm, but she was away from home. Mr White permitted us to ride over his grazing, and then off and away across the glorious moorland to drop down into Carrbrook. The old Roman Road usefully took us towards Greenfield and familiar routes to home.

P.S.Landscapes throughout my journeys bring memories flooding back, and I could shout aloud about them from the hilltops but who wants to listen? The ones who would love to listen are dead or scattered over the world. Treks make me happy and sad.

Edith.

Northumberland And Durham 1977

"Northumberland And Durham."
1976

DATE	OVERNIGHT ACCOMODATION	NOTES
June 6	Mankinholes Youth Hostel	B&B £2
June 7	Howarth Youth Hostel	B&B £5
June 8	Lothersdale Farm Guesthouse	B&B £5
June 9	Linton-in-Craven Youth Hostel	B&B £1
June 10	Kettlewell Youth Hostel	B&B £1
June 11	Hawes Youth Hostel	B&B £1
June 12	Keld Youth Hostel	B&B £1
June 13	Kirby Steven Farm Guesthouse Two days; evening meal	B&B £10
June 14	REST DAY	
June 15	Dufton Youth Hostel	B&B £1
June 16	Melmerby, Penrith Guest House Evening meal	B&B £5
June 17	Alston Youth Hostel	B&B
June 18	Haltwhistle Guest House Evening meal	B&B £5
June 19	Bardon Mill, Twice Brewed Inn Evening meal	B&B £5
June 20	Catton Allendale Guest house Evening meal	B&B £5
June 21	Hexham Youth Hostel	B&B £1
June 22	Alston Youth Hostel	B&B £1
June 23	Langdon Beck Youth Hostel Forrest-in-Teeside	B&B £1
June 24	Barnard Castle Youth Hostel	
June 25	Grinton Youth Hostel	B&B

June 26	Bellerby, Leyburn Cross Keys Inn	
	Evening meal	B&B £5
June 27	Horsehouse Guest house	
	Evening meal	B&B £5
June 28	Malham Buck Inn	
	Evening meal	B&B £8
June 29	Lothersdale Farm Guest house	
	Evening meal	B&B £5
June 30	Haworth Youth Hostel	
July 1	Hebden Bridge Guest house	
	Evening meal	B&B £5
July 2	Home	

"Northumberland And Durham."
1977

JUNE 6   Day 1

Leaving Crinkle Corner Cottage, to Delph and by way of Grange to Broadhead Noddle to Denshaw, then up A672 to Th'Owd Tup (Edith's name for The Ram's Head). Present day travellers can go up the bridleway at the side of Denshaw Church to Ralph's Farm, then Rough Hey Lane to the caravan site. This bridleway was impassable in 1977, and was a thorn in Edith's side. It was cleared too late for her to use it.

Left at the Ram's Head onto the R.U.P.P. known as Rape's Highway, passing Pythorne Reservoir on the left, following the old packhorse road, turn right through a gate leading to Rakewood. Under the motorway bridge to Hollingworth Lake, refreshments are available at the visitor centre.

Take the bridleway up to Syke and Clegg Moor, turning left on the wide track to Lydgate. Cross the minor road, then follow the track by the wall to the A58, where you turn left towards Littleborough.

A bridleway on the right leads down a leafy lane towards the canal, and through mill yards to Summit, where the A 6033 is crossed to a bridleway through disused quarry to estate roads leading to Calderbrook and the church. Turn right and follow this minor road to the A6033 and the old Toll House.

Left towards Todmorden, then right into Bottomly Road. Turn right over canal bridge and straight up the narrow, paved bridleway. A bridleway gate leads to a 'clangy' bridge bearing North West round Walsden Moor. After a number of farms, the bridleway becomes a stone causeway to Lumbutts Road; a right turn leads to Lumbutts and Mankinholes.

It is quite probable that Edith did not follow this route, but followed the now very busy A6033 to Walsden, then the minor roads to Mankinholes.

JUNE 7   Day 2

The bridleway below Stoodley Pike, leads to a lane to Hebden Bridge. Edith followed the A6033 through Pecket Well to the public house at Dike Nook. Due to present day traffic and re-opened bridleways it is possible to go over the packhorse bridge near the Tourist Information Centre, then up the cobbled lane turning right at the top to Hardcastle Craggs. A narrow paved bridleway at the side of a mill leads to Pecket Well and the A6033. Left up hill to Dike Nook, where a bridleway goes behind pub and down to B6141. Turn right to the cemetary, then left into lane to Haworth and Youth Hostel. Edith probably followed the main road right into Haworth

JUNE 8   Day 3

Lanes lead through Dockroyd, Dean Laithe, Slippery Ford, Crag Side, Brush to A6068. After crossing road more lanes to Carr Head and Upper Leys Farm and on to Lothersdale.

JUNE 9 Day 4

A track leads to Tow Top where a left, then right leads to Carlton. Right and first left to A59 Skipton. Edith used a side street to eventually pass the Hospital then took lane to B6265, following this North until it crosses a railway then track/lane on right running parallel with road to rejoin B6265 just south of Rylstone.

In the village a lane goes off on the right, passing the church, then rejoins B6265 for Cracoe and Lynton Youth Hostel.

JUNE 10 Day 5

Lanes leading into Grassington, then a minor road runs parallel with the B6160 through Conistone to Kettlewell Youth Hostel.

JUNE 11 Day 6

B6160 to Buckden, then a minor road through Langstrothdale leads to Hawes Youth Hostel.

JUNE 12   Day 7

Minor road over river leads to lanes over Abbotside Common and on to Thwaite,
The B6270 then leads to Keld Youth Hostel.

JUNE 13 Day 8

Edith followed the B6270 all the way to Kirkby Steven.

JUNE 14 Day 9

REST DAY

JUNE 15 Day 10

Edith followed the lanes that now form the Cumbria Cycleway through Soulby to the B6260 and into Appleby and on to Dufton Youth Hostel.

JUNE 16 Day 11.

Once again the lanes of the Cumbria Cycleway through Knock, Milburn, Blencarn to Skirwith, then on through Ousby to the Youth Hostel at Melmerby.

JUNE 17 Day 12

A686 all the way to Alston.

JUNE 18 Day 13
Lanes south of Whitfield Law rejoin the A689 at Slaggyford, then lanes through Knarsdale and Rowfoot lead to Haltwhistle.

JUNE 19 Day 14

B6318 and lanes lead to Bardon Mill.

JUNE 20 Day 15

Lanes lead south to the A686 and the B6303 to Catton.

JUNE 21 Day 16

Continuing south on B6303, then lanes past the Golf Club to Youth Hostel at Ninebanks.

JUNE 22 Day 17

Lanes along West Allen to Carr Shield, Coalcleugh, Nenthead and onto B6277 and Youth Hostel at Alston.

JUNE 23 Day 18

B6277 to Langdon Beck Youth Hostel.

JUNE 24 Day 19

B6277 to Newbiggin, then minor road to Middleton In Teesdale. From there the B6277 to Barnard Castle.

JUNE 25 Day 20

Minor roads over Hope Moor to Arkengarth Dale and on to Grinton Youth Hostel.

JUNE 26 Day 21

Minor road over Cogden Moor to Leyburn Moor and Bellerby.

JUNE 27 Day 21

A6108 to Layburn, then A684 west to cross river by church, then minor road south to Agglethorpe, Carlton and Horsehouse.

JUNE 28 Day 22

Continue on minor road to Kettlewell then B6160 south, then minor road to Arnecliffe and over Cowside to Malham Tarn and Malham.

JUNE 29 Day 23.

Minor roads through Kirkby Malham, Airton, Gargrave to cross A65 to minor roads to Broughton. A short section of A59 then minor road to Elsack and Lothersdale.

JUNE 30 Day 24

The reverse of June 8 Day 3.

JULY 1 Day 25

Reverse of June 7 Day 2 as far as Hebden Bridge.

JULY 2   Day 26

A646 to Mytholmroyd then B6138 to A58. West then to minor road to Lydgate, then bridleway over top of moor, through farmyard and over high level motorway bridge and down into Rakewood. Up hill on track to Rape's Highway and back to Ram's Head on A672. Down to Denshaw and over Heights to Delph and home.

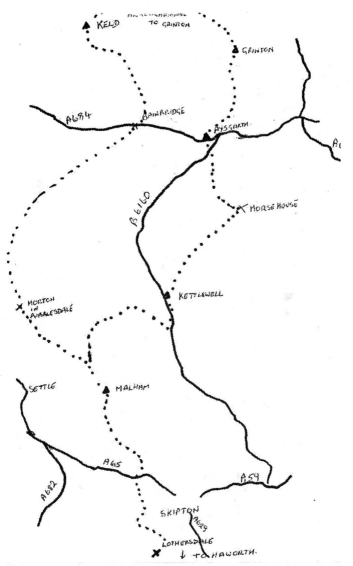

Yorkshire Dales And Fells 1978

"Yorkshire Dales And Fells."
1978

DATE	OVERNIGHT ACCOMODATION	NOTES
July 28th	Mankinholes Youth Hostel	£5
July 29th	Haworth Youth Hostel	£5.90
July 30th	Lothersdale Farm Guest House	£8
July 31st	Malham Farm Guest House	£9
August 1st	Horton-in-Ribblesdale Farm Guest House	£9
August 2nd	Bainbridge Guest House	£9
August 3rd	Keld Youth Hostel	£5.40
August 4th	Grinton Youth Hostel	£5.40
August 5th	Aysgarth Youth hostel	£5.40
August 6th	Horsehouse Thwaite Arms	£9
August 7th	Kettlewell Youth Hostel	£6
August 8th	Malham Farm Guest House	£9
August 9th	Lotherdale Farm Guest House	£8
August 10th	Haworth Youth Hostel	£5.90
August 11th	Mankinholes Youth Hostel	£5
August 12	Home Home	Lunch £2

An article by EDITH BOON

On Friday 28th as I set out casually in the usual manner on the nineteenth journey, I realised that it was the first for Janet and John, my companions and members of my local bridleways group. Now it is over, will they attempt another such journey, in spite of unfortunate happenings? I think they will.

All morning we travelled our nine to ten miles on the old familiar local romantic tracks; parts of 'Rapes Highway' used by me over a period of at least twenty years, still sinking slowly deeper into bog; a post and rail fence built across our 'highway' in my early riding days, forces one onto a sheep track running narrowly, but safely parallel to the way. (NOTE: during the 1990's the route was substantially repaired, and repairs are ongoing)

Eventually after a mile or so of this we passed through a gate on the right leaving 'Rapes' to follow yet another well-defined track to the works in the valley bottom. At this point a very steep track leads to a frightening moderate sized bridge across the M62.

Through the farmyard on the other side we reached Clegg Moor, this we crossed by a definite cart track between banks of heather and bracken. At Lydgate, the old Halifax Road is followed right to reach the new Halifax Road that crossed Blackstone Edge.

In search of lunch and grazing we turned left to the Moorcock. Here a small well grassed field is most convenient and Mrs.... soon had meals of trout, plaice and gammon prepared, also not neglecting to provide a pleasant sweet and much welcomed coffee.

We took our time as the horses must have two hours of grazing; during this time they certainly consumed enough to take them the next eight mile journey.

Tracks and lanes after lunch led us to the only two miles of road on our first day's trek. This was suffered patiently for most is ridden pleasantly on a grassy edge. Now for a steep climb up over a shoulder of rough grazing on grassy moor on a 'true' packhorse road. This was a thrilling experience; the pavement was still useable though crooked in places or hidden, not too deeply in a bog. (NOTE: this old route has been recently restored to its former glory and no longer is hidden in a bog.)

Lumbutts didn't seem far; then by using a short distance of farm and reservoir track we reached pretty Mankinholes Youth Hostel and nearby Mrs K .... 's grazing. Whilst in the evening we humans enjoy our 'human' contacts and exchange of news and views, the horses stoke up or rest easy for the long journey next day. I found great delight in meeting the farmer and his wife and the warden and family yet once again and I'm sure Janet and John in the future will go back to meet these new friends as gladly as I do.

The first journey over, what have we experienced to report to our friends of Bridleways Association and what comments have we collected to report to the engineers of our local authorities? Throughout our journey these engineers were in our minds, how we wished they could ride with us! If tracks were well preserved and gates well hung, how riders would enjoy their holiday, for far more can be seen of great beauty, scenery, plants and small animal life from horseback than from a car or from a bicycle Even more is seen by a rider than a person on foot. I think that at the end of a long journey of a fortnight we can honestly say that one gate in a hundred fastens well and is hung rightly and can therefore be opened and shut without dismounting. The tracks would live forever if the draining was supervised and kept in working order. Because of the spread of bog we are losing lovely riding ways. If these ways were supervised properly the walker and the cyclist would be much helped.

The horses were easily brought in and tacked up the next morning for they had learned the 'pastures new' routine and delighted in it. Mankinholes has a sign-posted bridleway, which after about 1 mile is lost in a shocking deep bog. This I knew about, but deemed it wise to reconoitre the evening before, in case the local authority had done something about it. No, it was still dangerous (NOTE: it has now been repaired) and a very kindly local woman allowed us to bypass the morass by using her private road and gate. The rest of London Road is passable but forces one onto a macadam road sloping downward and covered with a macadam aggregate so slippery that we had to dismount. Several times this situation occurred - the bridleway finished at a road covered with dangerous macadam, which if engineers were thoughtful could be surfaced with a non-slip aggregate.

After Horsehold it is necessary to ride on a very busy main road in Hebden Bridge, but very shortly a signposted bridleway takes one through pleasant woodland and eventually to Jackson Bridge. Now, after a mile of roadway, we were riding up Mr S ... 's driveway. There was suitable grazing, given a farmer's permission, and then another most remarkable experience. We enjoyed a delicious lunch in a Jacobean House crammed full of antique furniture, china etc with valuable pictures everywhere. The horses needed two hours here, and they were rather reluctant to leave the grazing.

Some road riding, and we were riding through the woods of Hardcastle Craggs. This day was sunny and hot and the flies were vile. Lovely tracks with stupid gates at frequent intervals led us from the deep wooded valleys to the open Haworth Moor. Do not think that all this distance was walked; - periods of trotting and cantering on grass were enjoyed for as long as the great heat allowed. This afternoon journey was long, and we arrived late at our nights grazing; however, friends everywhere, and we were given a lift to the Youth Hostel where we were welcomed and soon we were enjoying an evening meal. Janet relearned the art of YHA bed making!

YHA breakfasts are very satisfying and pleasant, but NOT the weather! We returned to the farm for the horses, and there we were lucky to be able to tack up indoors. Actually it wasn't a farm; the owner breeds heavy horses and his daughter owns ponies and even runs an annual show, which clashes with our Pony Club Open Show each year.

From Oakworth village we were soon on bridleways found through John's brilliant map reading. Again we found the Local Authority lacking in ideas as far as bridleways were concerned; suddenly there was a short iron post in the middle of the track, as it finished to enter a roadway. We carefully manouvered the horses by it, what if we had to turn back!! We would have been very annoyed, to say the least, and I don't think I can express what the horses would have felt. It was about this point that we found a mapped bridleway filled with stone walling; this meant a retracing of steps and from this point much road riding

Much apparent grassy edge is deceiving, so even a

horse won't use it. Local Authorities, would it cost so much to level about 2 feet of grass starting at the edge of the macadam? There could still be the necessary ditch and runnels if they were crossing the 'Horse track' at regular intervals.

This was Sunday, and only a half day journey. We finished on a field track that led into Woodhead Farmyard.

The horses were soon turned out and we went in search of a lunch in the village of Lothersdale. After a 'basket' lunch we returned to Woodhead Farm, which is on the Pennine Way. Mrs B.... fills her house nightly with Pennine Way walkers and this year most decided to give up and go home because the weather had been so inclement since starting out from Edale. The weather was so bad we settled in Mrs B's living room and Janet and John learned to know Mrs B. I knew her of old.

Monday was to be another long day, but with plenty of bridleways. We saddled up in miserable conditions and off we went down to Lothersdale Village to find the bridleway to lead us to the road to East Marton and lunchtime. At least it was fine by lunch and for the rest of the day.

The end of the bridleway from the Cross Keys at East Marton to Bank Newton was marred by the farmer's warped idea of farmyard protection.

At this point Edith's written article finishes and only rough notes remain.

EDITH'S NOTES

Mon July 31

Tied Dog!! (probably the farmer's warped ideas referred to above) Slippery roads. Gates - catches too low, bad hinges very rare passing thro without dismounting. Bridleways abandoned, to Malham - now for old familiar routes.

Tues Aug 1

The rain and wind continues endlessly. The limestone ---- Road between walls. Narrow cattlegrids gate- STRONG springs. Climbed to the tarn. Green carpet. Sad discovery- to be sadder.

Wed Aug 2

Phone to delay our journey to Bainbridge. CUT HAY! Phones Mrs K.. and delayed journey. Our good fairy John Torr Return to farm - vet- rest Horton in Ribblesdale. Swelling. Choice of two routes. Locked gates to set out on our long day.

Note: I believe Janet's horse went lame and had to be returned home to Oldham. Edith and John continued.

Thurs Aug 3

Trepidation till we discovered Janet and set out on our longest day. Passed Pennine Way walkers. Blew and rained - wet track. Basis of track mainly limestone.

Pennine Way at this point bridleway. Made good time on Roman Road   To Bainbridge and Shaw Cote.

Fri Aug 4

To Grinton. To Lands End. 'Robin' (John's horse) ate bird. Mrs K..... had walked John and G. Visited Keld YH to explain our absence.

Sat Aug 5

First by road edges - then venture upon mapped bridleway. The lovely limestone area. Old ways, soft green carpet covered. Wet point not troublesome. Castle Bolton then onto more trotting and cantering to Aysgarth YH and field.

Sun Aug 6

To Horsehouse - long stretch of green carpet again- cantered on and we strayed into old mine shaft remains - we were lost, turned back. Lost shoe, saw arrows. Thwaite Arms for night. Horses at Johnstones. Welcomed. 6miles grass, 2 miles road.

Mon Aug 7

Walked to Kettlewell - so much road edge - dared not try bridleways signposting not good enough. Home for box. Jacqueline solved our problem. Started home. Marvellous driving by John got us home.

Aug 8

Returned Malham.

Aug 9

Drove home visiting places where cancelling necessary.

"Through The Yorkshire Dales."
1978

My husband, John, and I undertook this journey for our holiday with Mrs. Boon in 1978. The three of us planned the trip together, beginning by studying O.S. maps of the area in the January and going on to research places to stay, accommodation for the horses etc. John and I benefited greatly from Edith's considerable previous experience of planning such trips, having wanted to do such a thing, but not knowing how to start, what the pitfalls were likely to be etc. Part of our planning entailed the three of us driving by car around the area of our planned route, to ensue that the bridleways and other tracks we intended to use were, in fact, passable - which several of them were not! We also made some attempt to get our horses fitter for the journey beforehand by doing some long day rides of 20 miles or so.

The horses were Coffee (John's 15.2 bay gelding, cobby type), Robin (my 14.1 light chestnut pony gelding) and Simon (a black gelding about 14.2, which Mrs. Boon rode. Mrs. Boon's Raven had died shortly beforehand and I think Simon was borrowed.)

This is a copy of notes I made after our return, with the intention of expanding them into a proper article - but, like so many plans, it never came to fruition! There are also a few photographs, somewhere!

Day 1, Friday, July 28

Home - Mankinholes Youth Hostel

Departure on time, from Ladcastle 10.00 a.m. to meet Mrs. B. at 10.30. Weather fine, hot. Lunch at Moorcock - met by Brenda - uncut hay field for horses.

Day 2, Saturday, July 29

Mankinholes - Haworth Youth Hostel.
Weather too hot, flies bad, especially in Cragg Vale. Lunch at Sutcliffe's. Horses refused to be caught - Simon's doing! Took long way round at Haworth to farm where horses spent night. Long walk to Youth Hostel!

Day 3, Sunday, July 30

Haworth - Lothersdale, Woodhead Farm (Mrs. Burnt - out's!)
Rain - saddled up in wet - Gillian let us use stables so at least under cover. Horses glad to come in. Miserable day - mainly roadwork. Blocked bridleway - had to find alt. route - slippery ford area. Reached farm at midday - woman objected to us going through next-door farm - O.K.'d with Burnops. Lunch at pub in Lothersdale. Farm chaos! Pennine Way walkers, campers! Afternoon - tack cleaning! Lump appeared on Coffee's off hind thigh - Insect bite? No pain so no worry.

Day 4, Monday, July 31

Lothersdale - Malham
Dry, dull, bright periods. Good riding. Lunch at East

(or West?) Marton - pub. Some great bridleways! But few signposted. Bad entrance though farm - should complain - couldn't negotiate alone. Mrs. B. stayed at Geldard's, us at Town Head Farm. Mrs. Moon had to go to funeral, so not really wanted, but still made welcome. Dinner at Lister's Arms - duck a l'Orange! Spoke to Pennine Way walkers coming "downhill" about route over Cam & Dodd Fells. Change of clothes at Malham.

Day 5, Tusday, August 1

Malham - Dub Cote Farm, Horton-in-Ribblesdale
Dry but cloudy. Good riding, but narrow gate on bridleway round Tarn. Made good time to Horton - woman stopped us to talk nr. Horton! Left horses at Glasgows' farm. Lunch at 3 Peaks cafe - Pennine Way stop. Wet afternoon.

Day 6, Wednesday, August 2

Weather fair. Disaster - Coffee's leg swelled up - returned to Glasgows' after 1 mile - called vet - 2 p.m. - kick - to be rested. Phoned J.T. (John Torr) - evening collected John & Coffee in horsebox. John stayed home, to return in car next day & meet us on main road between Cam Fell & Roman Road. Phoned Mrs. Keyes at Bainbridge to take us 1 day later. Stayed at Glasgows' 2nd night.

Day 7, Thursday, August 3

Missed Keld out. Horton - Bainbridge - Park House

(Shaw Cote?). To meet John at lunchtime.

Rain, cold, mist - worst day! Couldn't use Forestry road because of locked gates - complain! Forced to try unknown track! Chased by loose ponies on moors! Wet - stream unfordable - up to horses' bellies! Missed John on main road. Waited a while but too cold & wet - pressed on along Roman Road. Met John as approaching Bainbridge - straight to Molly Keyes' (John o' Groats to Land's End lady!). Horses tired, wet, hungry - good job had unexpected day's rest at Horton. Afternoon - to Keld in car to cancel & look at waterfalls - met same Pennine Way Walkers again! Molly Keyes could only take 2 lodgers - John went home to see Coffee after evening meal at Hawes. Ran over dog nr. Hawes - bump on nose - not serious.

Day 8, Friday, August 4

Re-planned route: Bainbridge - Grinton Youth Hostel

Cloudy, dry, misty on tops. Met 2 girls on holiday with horses nr. Grinton but riding out from base - went part of way with them. Many bridleways shown over Grinton Moors but couldn't find them! Arrived Grinton lunch-time - left horses at hostel - went to pub - eventually saw John passing!

John brought sausage rolls & pies for lunch - went to Reeth by car. Change of clothes at Grinton - no need to return later for cases - go in car now!

Day 9, Saturday, August 5

Grinton - Aysgarth Youth Hostel

Couldn't find bridleway over moors again - signposts needed! Cold, dull, cloudy. Good time & good riding to Castle Bolton. Bridleway to Carperby - indistinct in places - had to lift gate off hinges. Arrived Aysgarth lunchtime, met by John. Horses in Youth Hostel field. Motor bike rally on opposite! Lunch in pub. Germans arrived at Y.H. en masse!

Day 10, Sunday, August 6

Aysgarth - Horsehouse, Thwaite Arms.
Disaster. Cold, wet, windy. O.K. to Westburton & bridleway, then took wrong route (lack of waymarking) - lost on moors. Ended in bog, Simon threw shoe & broke hoof badly. Decided to turn back & find phone to contact John - saw arrows on stone - tried to find way again - signpost broken - saw farm & went to ask way - long way round but road smoother for Simon's hoof. Mrs. B. led Simon, I went ahead to find John at Horsehouse. Finally got horses to Arkleside - rang blacksmith - ill! To try again in morning. Corn feed for horses! (Only hard feed all trip which was done completely off grass)! Played dominoes with locals at Thwaite Arms! Sunday dinner: roast lamb, salad & cake!

Day 11, Monday. August 7

Horsehouse - Kettlewell Youth Hostel
Blacksmith still too ill. Considered boxing home but decided hills too steep & lanes too narrow & they wouldn't find us easily anyway! Rode to Kettlewell

mainly on grass. Made quite good time but no food at Youth Hostel so decided not to stay. Left horses at farm - tried to phone to arrange box - numerous difficulties - phone out of order - no change wrong numbers - no answer! Decided to drive home & arrange box!

Day 12, Tuesday, August 8

Journey abandoned (had done most of intended route!). John arranged to drive Rosebury's box. Collected horses. Returned by car for 1 last night at Malham!

"I remember parts of the journey very well, but other bits are very vague. Mrs. "Burnt-out's" at Lothersdale was a highlight (?), as was getting lost on Horsehouse Moor, and being chased by the ponies on Dodd Fell. Barbara (I can't remember her other name, but she had a grey horse which had navicular and was married to Gerald who was in T.V. - Barbara, I mean, not the horse) knew all about the farm at Lothersdale and thought it hilarious that we were going to go there. Someone else who might be helpful is Urszula Idziak, although I don't know if she went on any of "The Brigadier's" journeys.

During our journey with Mrs. B., we discovered why she always tried to memorise the route the night before - it was simply that she couldn't wear her glasses to map-read on horseback! She got very impatient with us when we tried to stop to look at the map! One of her pet hates was what she called "shoulder-gates". These were gates that were impossible to open without dismounting, which meant that she often had to walk quite a long way to find somewhere where she could climb up to re-mount, which she found rather difficult. Needless to say, I did most of the gate opening!

The planning before the journey was fascinating in itself. Apart from working out possible routes and places to stay, we needed to organise changes of clothes to be sent ahead and dirty clothes to be returned afterwards, so that we didn't have to carry too much. When she journeyed alone, Mrs. B. did all this by post, but on our journey we had the advantage of having access to the car.

Even though our journey sounds like a catalogue of mishaps, we thoroughly enjoyed it all and shall always see it as a journey of a lifetime. We couldn't have done it without Mrs. B., and I cannot see us doing it again, although we may dream."

Janet Slade
Sept 1998

Barbara Haigh

Dark and White Peak district

Edale from Bridleway to Hollins Cross   Dark Peak

Marsh and Marigolds   Spring in Dark Peak

Last bridleway to Mankinholes Youth Hostel...

Edith's first stop on journeys North

Paved bridleway above Walsden en route to Mankinholes

Causey Stone bridleway   Walsden to Mankinholes

The road to Mankinholes

Edith with "Sam"

Edith on "Sam" and Pauline Ramsden on "Kingfisher"
Photgraph courtesy of Enid Michaels

Edith on Grey Horse

Barbara Haigh

Peak District

Old Dam

House in Hartington

Bridleway above Ladybower

Shropshire and Wales

The Pound Inn   Leebotswood Shropshire

View towards Shrewsbury from Shropshire Plain

Youth Hostel   Capel- y- Ffin

Gospel Pass   Capel – y – Ffin

Welsh countryside   Ystrad Aeron

Barbara Haigh

Yorkshire Dales

Valley towards Thwaite

Waterfalls and cliffs

A house in the wilds above Natesby

Farmhouse at Langdon Beck

Lynton bridge and ford

Village of Buckden

Hubberholt

Deepdale

"Bambi" the caravanette used to research routes, parked outside Ninebanks Tower

"The Great Triangle."
1979
(A 70th Birthday Ride).

Prior to Edith's death, I spent quite some time with her putting on paper the route she took on the Great Triangle. The information I got from her, confirmed by notes and lines on her maps, gave me the route as planned in her living room at Crinkle Corner Cottage. The route was adjusted on a daily basis whilst on the trek, using local knowledge, and sometimes accompanied by local riders. I have included under each day's intinery any notes that Edith made, either on the maps or on her reminder cards for her lectures.

The maps she used were mainly the BARTHOLEMEWS NATIONAL MAPS SERIES 1:100,000, which are intended for motorists and do not give bridleways etc but have the advantage of being smaller than O.S. maps

SUN 17 June 1979

Delph to Denshaw, and a sending off from the members of West Pennine Bridleways Association, at their annual show; then by way of Castleshaw to Standedge and the road facing the Great Western Inn to Marsden; then a right turn into the Wessenden Valley (which at this time was under dispute as it was classified as footpath, but, due in part to Edith, was in 1995 reclassified as bridleway). Up to the A 635 and B&B.

NOTES: Simon at Harden Green Farn and missing his pals. Invitation to dinner on return. Fish and chips.

MON 18 June

Bridleway to Flush House passing Digley reservoir, then lanes downhill to Holmbridge and A6024. Turn right then left after church bearing immediately right to Brownhill reservoir. At Crossleys Plantation left, and bridleways past Harden Quarries to Harden and Dunford Bridge.

Through Townhead and Carlecotes to the cross roads to B6106 and then right to Weer. Cross A628 to Ecklands then right and left to A628, left on minor road to Langsett Youth Hostel.

NOTES. Lunch - usual welcome and help at Stanhope Arms. Bought crop from daughter at Wagon and Horses. Fell off - girth not tight enough.

TUES 19 June

Through Upper Midhope on lane past Barnside Moor to Ewden, Agden Bridge, Bole Edge Plantation to Strines Inn for lunch

Right onto A67, left A6013, right Yorkshire Bridge, left Thornhill, right Aston, to Hope; cross A625 then lanes into Castleton and Youth Hostel.

NOTES. Lunch, small patch grass. Helpful landlord- knew his horses- good drawing ponies.

Castleton - pastured with another gelding. Blacksmith at 7am one nail changed.

WED 20 June

Hope, then past Pindale Farm to Roman Road and

the top bend above Peak Forest. Cross A623 then via Potluck and Wheston to Millers Dale. Through Priestcliffe to cross A6. Lanes to Buxton Youth Hostel.

NOTES. Lunch- cantered track to Peak Forrest - welcome at farm. Buxton Youth Hostel new warden, helpful. Rode with his child on morning. Used field opposite Foxlow Lodge-saw no-one.

THURS 21 June

Lanes and Tissington Trail to Royal Oak Hurdlow. Short day

NOTES. No lunch necessary. Garage proprietor could not take joke!! No petrol only directions. Sterndale. Welcome at Royal Oak. NO PARCEL. Lovely evening party for little boy. Local press on leaving looking forward to return. Offered to send on parcel.

FRI 22 June

Tissington Trail and lanes to Hartington Youth Hostel.

NOTES. Pleasant down trail. Saw Duke of Edinburgh teacher training girls Hartington. Long chat with retired couple on seat in sunshine - wise comments on world. Lovely old hall. Horse could not be got nearer, awkward. Interested owner.

SAT. 23 June

Tissington Trail to Fenny Bently then lanes to Ilam.

NOTES. Back on trail. People recognise me and chat. Rode with mother and daughter towards Izaac Walton. At last found smith. Field near another lovely hall as Youth Hostel. Afternoon tea with interesting couple, woman climbed, both camped Hope to do a long distance coast walk Helpful next morning. Ready for early bed.

SUN 24 June

Lanes through Blore, Latham Hall, Calton, Waterhouses, Caulden, Lanehead to Ipstone.

NOTES. Making for Ipstone, Heavy rain, baulking. Much main road. Frogham unnecessary. Found lane to farm with cattle grid and no gate. Grey Welsh pony in bridleway. Adventure in field with 30 bullocks. A great welcome and much drying of wet clothes. Mixed with family visitors (Jewish salesman) daughter and husband, boy and girl. Much comment on 'World and the Young etc"

MON 25 June

B5053 to Froghall, right A52, left A521 through Kingsley Holt. Right past The Booth Farm to A522. Right and left for Godleybrook, Dilhorne, Blythbridge. Past the station to B5029 and the junction of A520 and A5005 then lane to Barlaston.

NOTES Escort of 4 girls. Neighbour's cattle grid had no gate so followed ponies through ditch. Left me at canal. Sails up canal with meals. Simon would not take the overflow in spite of help from stranger and canal boat horse with tow rope; off-putting. Went back to Froghall. Looked for blacksmith at Cheadle, false alarm - too old and other not at home.

Found "The Planets" so very kind. Lunch for me and rest for Simon. At last set off for Barlaston. Farmer introduced me to bridleways, very wet and sandy due to tractors. Mrs Dickson missed me because I used these bridleways. Found me near her home and took me to Mrs Chambers. Simon happy - so was I very soon. Bath and great comfort! Business took Mrs Dickson away. But son and daughter-in-law were very entertaining. Jean had travelled by rail, recounted adventures. So much relevant discussion in this home.

Local press at Mrs Chamber's home. Sorry to leave so congenial atmosphere. So much was arranged by phone. Blacksmith was awaiting at Eccleshall, thought we could make it. Though shoes were very thin; limestone roads of Derbyshire were very slippy and caused wear.

TUES 26 June

Past station to A34 Left and first right to A51, right turn and cross M6. First right past Sandyford Farm and at 'Y' junction bear left through Sturbridge to A519 and Eccleshall.

NOTES. Swinnerton no use for lunch, so pressed on. Reached blacksmith at Eccleshall at 2pm. Smartly done by young blacksmith.

Made comfortable at Kings Arms. Landlady, Mrs

Rollit, became interested. Quite a character. Pleasant evening meal etc. Simon found grazing in orchard field next to skewbald gelding. together by morning. Young lady who helped in pub went for Simon in morning.

WED 27 June

Lanes all day passing Cop Mere, Bishops Offley, Doley, Cheswardine, Wistanwick, Heathcote, Stoke Upon Tern to Hodnet.

NOTES. Across country to Hodnet. Much road. Longed for Local Authorities to level off work done at roadside edges. Look up map to revise. Lunch - manager absent through accident, no field. Butcher offered to put Simon with sheep. Young lady helped. No help in morning, much gate climbing. Good hotel accommodation- T.V in room. Bath. No need to sit in on disco!!

THURS 28 June

A53 right to Hopton, then lane on left to Stanton Upon Hine Heath, continue to Moreton Corbet then B5063 to Shawbury. Right A53 and first right into lane. Right into R.U.P.P for Shawbury Heath to Astley. Cross A53 into bridleway to Sundorne Farm.

NOTES. Tedious road but lot of edge. Reached Sundorne Castle quite pleasantly though seemed long way.

FRI 29 June   REST DAY

SAT 30 June

B5062 to A5112, sharp left onto A5112 at Underdale, then minor road along river to A5. Right onto A5. cross railway, left into A49 and immediate right to minor road to Belle View. Cross A5 near church and cemetery then follow minor road to Newbold, Longden, Wrenthall and Youth Hostel at Bridges.

NOTES. Much road work but very straight to Bridges. People waving from cars and stopping to chat. Happens ever day now. Shropshire hill country very beautiful. Simon in field across from hostel. Warden helpful. Met Duke of Edinburgh girls again.

SUN 1 July

Ratlinghope and Burway Hill to Church Stretton, then B4371 Wall Under Heywood, then about a mile to bridleway to Wilderhope Youth Hostel.

NOTES. Marvellous over Long Mynd. Cardine Mill valley too steep, Burway difficult. Met little man outside Church Stretton who recognised me. Pleasant lunchtime.
Afternoon 2 miles of bridleway!! Shocking gates. Welcome at Youth Hostel, a marvellous manor house.

MON July 2

Bridleway to lane then left down to B4368. Right then left into lane to Tugford. Bridleway to R.U.P.P and Clee St Margaret, then lane to Stoke St

Millborough. At 'T' junction left then bridleway to
B4364. Left then right to Youth Hostel at Wheathill.

*NOTES. Wilderhope to Wheathill between Brown
Clee and Titterstone Clee.*

*Through the valley of the Clee the flies - NOT
ordinary black flies but ugly thick brown horse flies.
What an experience in the lovely village of Clee St
Margaret remarkable village with a elongated ford at
which Simon drank copiously, but the horse flies had
already started to drive him almost mad. Couldn't find
farmer at all (busy haymaking) At last released him
from his tack and put him in the Post Mistress's patch,
very tiny and full of nettles and flies!! Did not settle
and in a few moments had put his foot through sheep
netting. The Post Mistress was not pleased.*

*An old villager receiving his pension helped me to
release him. No damage done, but I left as quickly as I
could. Through rich arable and wooded country.
Simon was still awkward when he had arrived, now in
the cool at 8pm he is content and so am I. In a very
primitive hostel, no food provided, but a hostel shop
satisfied my simple wants - fish fingers, bread and
butter and milk to drink and Shredded Wheat for my
breakfast. MUST find a lunch place tomorrow.*

*Warden's family interested - daughter and son-in-law
both teachers. Farmer beef and sheep, but NOT hill
farmer. Soil here rich and red. First wheatlands out from
Wales. All Welsh border country very attractive.*

TUES 3 July

Bridleway and lanes to Cleestanton, Bitterly,

Angelbank, Knowbury, Snitton, Lower Ledwyche and Youth Hostel at Ludlow.

NOTES. Left early and met lollypop woman, helped with crossing. Lunch at Charleton Arms (private room for tack). Lovely farm for Simon. Changed at Youth Hostel, sent off parcel and visited laundrette and dry cleaners. Warden has ridden.

WED 5 July

Lanes to the Serpent, Middleton then A4105. Right and first left and lanes to Stoney Cross, Laysters Pole,

cross A4112 then lanes to Whyle, Puddleton and Hatfield Court.

NOTES. Kept going so arrived early. Bridleway good, gates horrid. Splendid welcome, field , water etc.

THURS 5 July REST DAY

Taken out to explore by hostess.

FRI 6 July

Lanes to A417 at Saffrons Cross then lanes to Sutton St Nicholas. The A4103 and A465 to Tupsley, Hereford.

NOTES. 70th BIRTHDAY WEEKEND.
Moved to Hereford and friends. Brought in Mr Jackson's hay. Dinner with Miss Noble from Argentine. Woman's Hour secretary brought cake.

SAT 7 JULY

NOTES. Shopping in Hereford for maps. Met friends for lunch home produce from fabulous garden. Miss Brath took us home in her campervan.

SUN 8 July

NOTES. To the Garfitts. Mr G came in BIG car. Simon - impressed. Much conversation. Mark arrived rival pet subjects (vintage cars or tales of Monte Carlo)   Lovely meal - elegance- two corgis. Dozed in garden under apple tree. Mr G nipped nail, off to Hereford hospital for anti tetanus. Supper and tales of old happenings.

MON 9 July

B4224 Mordiford, then lanes Priors Frome, Checkly, and Rushall Youth Hostel.

NOTES: The best riding day yet. Miss Brash escorted me down two or three overgrown bridleways with the badly hung gates. After an hour Miss Brash returned. I rode on to "Foley Arms" where I was met by Miss Noble on 'Dick', welsh cob thoroughbred cross, who looked a lovely ride. More bridleways over hills, woodland. Great views, on way to an impressive ranch. Simon got a deep bed and clover hay, oats and bran. Tackroom etc. VERY IMPRESSIVE. Perfection.

Impressive lunch. EVERYTHING home grown, cream from Jersey cow, friends exchange beef pork, great bottle of sherry for judging a show (dressage) Miss Noble ex dressage competitor (against Lorna Johnston etc) Much agreement over horsey and world problems. Miss Noble known marvellous horses. I questioned her about riding in the Argentine and we talked about "westerns". When it was time to move on Miss Noble used her western saddle on thoroughbred cross Arab - youngster would never make a dressage horse- Should TB cross Cleveland bay be encouraged? Would have loved more riding in these hills together, was invited back to do so.

Miss Noble took me via hill bridleway to Rushill Youth Hostel. Sadly said goodby to Miss Noble. Simon soon in large orchard field. Simple grade hostel, but very pleasant, young people, walkers and cyclists.

TUES 10 July

Lanes Much Marcle, cross A449 then lanes Windcross, Broom Green, and across the M50 to Ryton, Redmarley D'Aritot, Staunton and Corse.

NOTES. Visited historic Chartist bungalows.

WED 11 July

B4231 Tirley and Lower Apperly and Farmers Arms. Lanes Deerhurst Walton, cross M5 to Stoke Orchard, Bishops Cleeve, Woodmancote then A46 to Cleeve Hill Youth Hostel.

THURS 12 July

Lanes through Corndean Hall, Charlton Abbots,

Whittington, across A40 to Kilkenny, across A436 to Hilcot, across A435 to Colesborn, across A417 to Winston and on to Duntisbourne Abbots Youth Hostel.

FRI 13 July

Lanes crossing A429 to Ewen, Poole Keynes, Oaksey. Crudwell. Across A429 to Long Newnton, across A4014 then minor roads past lakes to Shipton Moyne, Easton Grey, across B4040 and lane south of Sherston to Alderton.

NOTES. Journey too long. Phoned hostess and was met on Fosse Way and changed route Simon not well. Vet called. Possible allergy or teeth.

SAT 14 July

Lanes to Littleton across M4 then B4135 Burton Hinton and lanes to Abson, and Youth Hostel Wick.

SUN and MON 15 and 16 July. REST DAYS.

NOTES. Went sight seeing with friends visiting Bristol and Bath.

TUES 17 July

Lanes to Bitton, then A431 and A417 to Keynsham. Lanes to Woolard and Hunstrete, across A368 and A39 to Farmborough then lanes to Timsbury, Paulton crossing A362 to Midsomer Norton.

NOTES. Simon in very large field. Could not find him. T.V. interview.

WED 18 July

B 3855 and A 367 to Stratton On The Fosse, then lanes to Holcombe and Nettlebridge. Across A367 then lanes to Gurney Slade and Croscombe and North Wootton. The A39 Glastonbury, then lanes to Butleigh Wootton and Street Youth Hostel.

NOTES. Rode bridleway over Glastonbury Tor.

FRI 20 July

Lanes through Butleigh, Barton St David, Keinton Mandeville, Charlton Adam, Charlton Mackrell, to night stop at Somerton.

SAT 21 July

Lanes passing through Pitney, Huish, Muchelney, Ash, Tintihull, to overnight at Montacute.

NOTES. Simon re-shod.

SUN 22 July

Lanes and roads through Odcombe, East Coker, Stoford, to Bradford Abbas.

NOTES. Left Simon and went to Yeovil by train to visit brother and family.

MON 23 July to THURS 26 July: REST DAYS.

NOTES. Spent time with brother and family talking and sight seeing.

FRI 27 July

Lanes and roads through Hackett, Yetminster, Chetnole, Leigh, to Manor House at Holnest.

SAT 28 July

Across A352 and into lanes through Holwell. Across B3143 and through Kings Stag, Bulbarrow Hill, Wooland, Okeford Fitzpaine to overnight at Child Okeford.

SUN 29 July

Lanes through Hambledon Hill, Sutton Waldron, Cranborne Chase, to night halt at Tarrant Hinton.

MON 30 July

Mainly lanes through Tarrant Launeston, Tarrant Monkton, Manswood, Moor Crichel, Gussage All Saints, to Youth Hostel at Cranborne.

TUES 31 July

Lanes through Edonsham, Pinnocks Moor, to Somerly House.

NOTES. T.V. interview for 'South Today.'

WED 1 Aug

Crossing A338 lanes north to Frogham.

NOTES. New Forest ponies in horrible condition. Do they need worming? Saw herds of donkeys. Simon hates them. PROBLEMS.

THURS 2 Aug

Tracks through New Forest to Riding School at Canada.

FRI 3 Aug

Through West Wellow and East Wellow across A27 and bear right to B3084 and on to Timsbury then lanes to Braisfeld.

SAT 4 to MON 6 Aug   REST DAYS

NOTES. Visiting cousins in Romsey and Portsmouth.

TUES 7 Aug

Lanes to Hursley across A3090 then lanes to Olivers Battery and Winchester Youth Hostel.

WED 8 Aug

Lanes going East Ashley, Little Somborne and Stocksbridge and the A30. After crossing the river right turn into lanes to Longstock and St Johns Cross. Across A343 to Abbotts Ann then lanes to Weyhill. Across A303 Penton Mewsey, then lanes to Wildhern Youth Hostel.

THURS 9 Aug

Lanes to Upton, Linkenholt, Combe, Forbury, Iinkpen, Ham, Shalbourne and overnight at Great Bedwyn.

FRI 10 Aug

Through Savernake Forest to Marlborough.

SAT 11 Aug

Lanes to Mildenhall and The Ridgeway to Wanborough.

SUN 12 Aug

Ridgeway to Wantage.

MON 13 Aug

Ridgeway to Streatley.

NOTES. On Independent Radio programme with local vet, who answers listeners' queries on vetinary matters.

NEW INFORMATION:- From this point it is possible to join the Midshires Way, a leafleted and way-marked route for walkers, cyclists and horse riders all the way to Stockport near Manchester.

TUES 14 Aug

B4526 to A4074. Crossing the A road into lanes to B481 at Rotherfield Peppard, then across 'B' road into lanes to Henley On Thames.

WED 15 Aug

A423 Assendon, then B480 and right turn into lanes to Fawley and Fingest. Cross M40 to A40 to West Wycombe and Youth Hostel at Bradenham.

THURS 16 Aug

Lanes to A413 then cross 'A' road to Huntsgreen and Youth Hostel at Lee Gate.

FRI 17 Aug

Lanes to Chivery and Ridgeway and lanes to

Ivinghoe Youth Hostel.
NOTES Ridgeway is a FOOTPATH!!!

SAT 18 Aug

B489 then lanes to Little Gaddensden, Great Gaddensden and Gaddensden Row. Cross Ml to Redbourne and overnight stop at Harpendenbury.

SUN 19 Aug

Lanes to Hatching Green then across A6 to Nomansland and friend at Coleman Green.

MON 20 Aug

Cross Al(M) south of Welwyn Garden City and on to B195. Lanes lead to B158 then more lanes to Berkhampstead. Cross A10 to Broxborne and lanes to Royden and Youth Hostel at Harlow.

NOTE. Met local rider who took me onto old railway track to Harlow Youth Hostel. Simon overnight in Pets Corner.

TUES 21 Aug

B182 Hatfield Heath

NOTES. Got trailer lift to Colchester

WED 22 Aug to SUN 26 Aug REST DAYS
Stayed with friends in Colchester.

MON 27 Aug

Lanes through Little Tey, Great Tey, Earls Colne, Little Mapleshead, Great Mapleshead and on to Youth Hostel at Castle Hedingham.

TUES 28 Aug

Crossing A604 to Sible Hedingham, then lanes to Wetherfield and Finchingfield. Then B1053 and Great Stampford and Radwinter. Lanes to Wimbush and Bears Hall to Youth Hostel at Saffron Waldon.

NOTES. Met friend I had not seen for 30 years. Much talk.

WED 29 Aug

B1052 Linton and Balsham, then lanes via Great Shelford and Little Shelford to Simon's overnight stop, off the A410, at Harsten Equestrian Centre. Cambridge Youth Hostel for me.

NOTES. Visited lovely colleges and went behind the scenes.

THURS 30 Aug REST DAY

FRI 31 Aug

Lanes to Haslingfield across A603 to Little Eversden, Great Eversden, Kingston Bourne, across A45 to Knapwell. Across A604 to Fenstanton, across A1096 to Hemingford Grey and Youth Hostel at Houghton Mill.

SAT 1 Sept

Cross A1123 to B1090 Abbots Ripton then A1 to Sawtry. Lanes lead to Glatton, Denton and overnight stop at Warmington.

NOTES. Farmer's wife had hunter, daughter pony. Family introduced me to gamekeeper, very interesting. Got trailer lift to "Haycock" at Wansford. Old stable satisfactory. Had lunch at "George", Stamford, great welcome at Burghley horse trials.

SUN 2 Sept

Cross A605 then lanes to Tansor, Cotterstock, Glepthorn, Southwick, Apethorn, Kings Cliffe and night at Wansford.

NOTES. Bad roads am. Got lift: see above notes.

MON 3 Sept.

A47 and lanes Southorpe and Barnack, then B1443 Stamford.

TUES 4 Sept.

Ermine Street to Tickencote, then lanes towards Exton, Burley and night at Oakham.

WED 5 Sept.

Lanes to Brooke, Braunston, Knossington, Somerby and overnight at Leesthorpe Stables.

THURS 6 Sept.

Lanes to Little Dalby and Great Dalby. A607 to Kirby Bellars, then lanes and A6006 to Asfordey. More lanes to Saxelbye and Wartnaby, to overnight at Old Dalby.

NOTES. Leicestershire:- Allen's of Brooke Priory to meet me at Chatsworth Horse Trials. The Tarrant's at Leesthorpe know Saddleworth. Mumford Smith's race horse once at Diggle.

Melton Mowbray lunchtime for pork pie. Visited army remount depot and Vets' School. Simon set of shoes at Farriery School. Met Press.

FRIDAY 7 Sept

Lanes crossing A46 Willoughby On The Wold, Wysall and Bunny.

NOTES. Bunny Wood very pretty. Main road at Bunny horrid.

SAT 8 Sept

Lanes via Hotchley Hill, Cotham, Kingston On Soar and Kegworth, and then keeping east of M1. Lanes to Sawley. B6540 to Long Eaton, then B6002 to Sandiacre and B5010 to Risley for night.

SUN 9 Sept

Cancelled visit to Ainsworth to help out at local Gymkhana.

MON 10 Sept.

Lanes to Stanton By Dale, and Dale, across A6096 then lanes to Stanley. Across A608 to Breadsall and Breadsall Priory, and on to Little Eaton. Lanes via Edgehill and A6 to Duffield, then lane to Hazelwood and night stop at Shottlegate.

NOTES. Long day to farm, where Simon had rich grazing.

TUES 11 Sept

Lanes to Shottle and Spout, across B5035 to Bolehill and Middleton.

WED 12 Sept.

High Peak Trail to Friden.

THURS 13 Sept.

High Peak Trail to Royal Oak, Hurdlow.

FRI 14 Sept

Lanes through Earl Sterndale, then B5053 towards Buxton turning off for lanes to Hapurhill and Burbage, then lanes and tracks past White Hall Centre to Chapel en le Frith.

SAT 15 Sept.

Lanes through Chinley then bridleway over moor to Far Phoside, and down lanes into Hayfield.

SUN 16 Sept.

Lanes and tracks to Rowarth, then over Matley Moor to Monks Road, then down steep hill to Charlesworth, and drag hunt kennels.

NOTES. Cheshire. Slippery roads.. Good grazing for Simon at Hayfield. Met Peak Pony Club members who led me to hunt stables. Saw hounds fed. Looked well kept, so was I. Head girl kind and washed and groomed Simon for his homecoming.

MON 17 Sept.

Via Mottram and A6018 to Roe Cross, then tracks to Brushes, Sun Green, Carrbrook, Noonsun Hill and

Greenfield, then disused railine bridleways via Uppermill and Delph Donkey.   HOME!!!!!

WONDERFUL CELEBRATION.

THE GREAT TRIANGLE LECTURES

At the completion of the Great Triangle Ride, Edith set out on the Great Lecture Trail; a task which would have killed many a strong person. Edith was 70 years old, did not drive, and travelled to most of her lecture venues on public transport. Occasionally a friend would take her in a car, but Edith's usual mode of transport, when not on her horse, was either bus or train. The list of venues makes interesting reading, and although many places are close to or in the Oldham area, others, e.g. Gisburn and Bolton, are quite a journey by public transport.

The type of group who booked her is also interesting, from Ladies circles to Wine making Groups and retirement Associations.

1979

Oct 11th	Farmers Ladies Circle Greenfield
Oct 24th	West Pennine Bridleways
Oct 31st	Saddleworth Young Farmers
Nov 21st	Young Wives, Greenfield Methodist
Nov 27th	Delph Methodist Ladies Fellowship
Dec 5th	Fairfield High School for Girls

1980

Feb 12th	Saddleworth Forum
Feb 18th	Greenfield Methodist Ladies Fellowship
Feb 20th	Friends of Oldham Art Gallery
March 2nd	Bridleways Conference Gisburn

March 4th   Greenfield Congregational Over 60's
March 12th   Delph Senior Citizens
March 13th   Saddleworth Ladies
April 10th   Wine Makers Grotton
April 15th   Holy Trinity Women's Guild Oldham
April 16th   Saddleworth Church
April 22nd   Women's Institute Park Bridge
April 29th   St John's Girls Cadets Hope Derbyshire
May 12th   Oldham Ladies
May 15th   Mothers' Union Crumpsal Manchester
May 20th   Oldham Rambling Club
May 28th   Women's Unionists
May 29th   Ladies Scouthead Church
July 2nd   Probus Club Oldham
July 20th   N.H.R Burnedge
Sept 16th   Holy Trinity Waterhead Oldham
Oct 1st   Trinity Methodist Ladies Sect. Royton
Nov 15th   Prestwich Methodist Wednesday Ass.
Dec 11th   Reform Church Oldham
Dec 12th   Werneth Low Riding Club Hyde

1981

Jan 28th   Narrow Boat Canal Soct.
Feb 3rd   Young Farmers Oldham
Feb 4th   Retired Teachers Oldham
Mar 3rd   Inner Wheel AGM Oldham
Mar 25th   Young Ladies Royton
April 21st   Hope Ladies
May 6th   St. Annes Ladies
May 21st   Sports Council AGM
May 27th   Hesketh Bank Women's Inst.
June 8th   Chadderton Congregational.

July 7th	Townswomen's Guild Uppermill
July 16th	Delph W.I.
Aug 20th.	Mothers' Comm Centre Oldham
Aug 26th.	ARC General Meeting Uppermill
Sept 21st	Ashton Methodist Ladies
Oct 1st	Annual Dinner Stanley Lodge
Oct 16th	Annual Dinner B & P Union Club
Oct 27th	Norweb Penshioner's
Oct 28th	W.I Charlesworth
Nov 19th	P.T.Ass. Girls Grammar School
Nov 24th	D of E Presentation

1982

Feb 25th	Chadderton and Royton Ladies Circle
Mar 2nd	Moorside Methodist
Mar 9th	Bolton Ladies Circle
Mar 17th	Mid Weekers
Mar 22nd	St Georges Stalybridge
April 27th	Riding Club Clitheroe
May 6th	Limeside Methodist Ladies
June 18th	Heald Green Ladies
July 6th	St. Paul's Flats Sheltered Housing
July 7th	Oldham & Dist. Hospital
July 13[th.]	Heald Green
Sept 14th	Greenacres Cong. Ladies
Sept 13th	Woolworth's Retirement Ass Castleton

The list totals 64 lectures to a very diverse audience. Edith always stressed that age was no barrier to adventure, and in fact it could well be an advantage as time no longer matters and there is no longer the call of employment to prevent people getting on with the interesting things in life.

"Hostelling News."
Two Dozen Hostels
An article by Edith Boon

After being a walking hosteller for many years, I took to hostelling on horseback. I was born with a desire to ride journeys on horseback, and in my childhood, when walking tracks with my family, I daydreamed of the time when I would actually ride these tracks.

I nurtured my desire until 1946, when, after buying my first horse, I organised a fortnight's holiday on horseback, using hostels for my accommodation. The wardens, at my request, would include the name and address of nearby farmers with my booking receipt. I then wrote to a farmer about grazing for my horse for the night in a well-fenced field. I nearly always received a favourable reply.

My 35 years of holidays on horseback had begun. Mostly I set out from home, and organised a circular tour into North Lancashire, Yorkshire or Derbyshire. At that time I could use the railway to help me to the Welsh Border so that I could tour Mid Wales.

Another great desire was to ride a really long journey with a purpose. My horse and I would visit all my friends and relations, some of whom I hadn't seen for many years. I actually waited to carry out this from seven years to seventy. In 1979, on June 17th, I set out on a tour of England with my horse Simon. We travelled 777 miles, and arrived back home on Sept 17th. I slept in just over 70 beds, 24 of them Youth

Hostel beds, and I spent my 70th birthday on the 7th day of the 7th month near Hereford.

I called my journey 'The Great Triangle'. Setting out from home, (near Delph, a Saddleworth village in the Pennines between Manchester and Huddersfield) I made for Yeovil, my most south easterly point, and then east to Colchester, my most south westerly point, and from there rode northwards home.

As a Youth Hostels Association Life Member, I applied for accommodation to all possible Hostels that fitted into that triangular shape, and filled in where necessary with Guest Houses, farms and Riding Establishments, wherever I could stay. Of course, I wrote to all my friends and relations also, and before setting out I had fixed up my 92 nights. I chose to spend a week with my brother and his family, and a week with friends at Colchester. There were also several other rest days for Simon's sake.

On my daily travels I used bridleways and endless miles of English lanes, meandering through the world-famous variety of our English country scenes. It proved to be an epic journey; because of my age, and the distance to be covered, the media took a great interest. I was visited by the local press for copy and photographs at several Hostels. When being interviewed for Radio or T.V. I made much of the fact that I rested pleasantly many nights of the tour at Youth Hostels, and told how, in order to keep my pack weight down, I booked Hostel meals, which I find very appetising and good value for money. Only in three cases was the situation such that the warden could not help me with the catering for my horses.

On the first day when all the farewells had been said, there was only time for a half-day ride which was quite fast on attractive Pennine tracks. The second night was spent at Langsett Hostel, which I had often visited before.

On the third day I enjoyed the landscape, reservoir-filled Pennine valleys, sweet with the scent of hawthorn, enhanced by the colourful rhododendrons set against the dark pines. In making for Castleton, I was able to off track in order to rest Simon, and I lunched at the Strines Inn. The warden at Castleton had put me in touch with a woman who owned horses, so Simon was suitably accommodated there.

The ride up steep-sided Winnote Pass was one of the joys of the journey to Buxton Hostel. At the lunch break, Simon was welcomed by my old friend the farmer's wife, and I was welcomed by the family at the pub in the village of Peak Forest. In Derbyshire there are many defined bridleways and trails made available by the Authorities, using the old rail tracks. I left the Tissington Trail to visit Hartington and Illam Hostels.

At every Hostel there was much talk in the evenings, and everywhere starry-eyed young ladies, who rode a little at home, longed to come with me.

Accommodation in Shropshire was partly covered by four Hostels, Bridges, Wilderhope, Wheathill and Ludlow. Again interesting scenic variety, this time through an area having attractive historic buildings. The Association is doing a splendid job in helping to preserve our inheritance. How do wardens find the time to help visitors to appreciate the buildings? I visited Wilderhope in the early 50's, but how improved its condition is now.

Coming from a rather barren area agriculturally, there was much to observe on my journeys between Rushall, Cleeve Hill and Duntisbourne Hostels. The lovely sunshine was ripening the fat ears of wheat, but to see hop fields, and, even more exciting, a vineyard with its English wine factory was splendid. Things did not seem to go quite so smoothly as usual at Cleeve Hill, but the Warden found time to help the 'old lady'.

Street, on its hilltop, introduced me to a view of the 'moor'; to me a strange title for that flat ditch-drained area of Somerset. 'Moor' at home means impassable black peat bog on a flat hill-top.

After visiting my brother and his family at Yeovil, I made for the contrasting riding of the New Forest, the gateway being Cranbourne Hostel. Here the Warden and his wife found time to show a keen interest in my unusual mode of travel. The local press was invited, and I was delighted to tell how very glad I was to turn to the Y.H.A. for comfortable and pleasantly decorated resting places.

In the Forest I stayed with friends, riding eventually on The Ridgeway Path. At last I was riding on one of the most famous ancient tracks with its twenty miles of defined bridleway, where a local rider and I took advantage of the public gallops. From there, I made my way to the series of Hostels which run from the Thames to the beautiful wooded Chilterns: Streatley, Henley, Bradenham, Lee Gate, Ivinghoe and Harlow. All so different from each other, but each attractive in its own way.

At Streatley I found accommodation for Simon on arrival, for there was none planned. Luckily a Vet, who lived near the Hostel, found him some good grazing. I went with the Vet to an Independent Radio Station, and was interviewed by the D.J. before the Vet gave his regular talk on the care of pets.

At Henley, Simon was grazing near a campsite. At

Bradenham I had to find stabling at a Riding School 1.5 miles away. There was a considerate farmer near Lee Gate, and at Ivinghoe, a woman who bred Arabs fed Simon well, for I found him full of energy the next day. At Harlow Simon grazed at Pets' Corner in the park! Variety is the spice of life!

At Colchester it was evident that Simon knew we had turned north towards Home. In crossing the arable counties of Essex and Cambridgeshire, I used the Hostels of Castle Hedingham. Saffron Walden, Cambridge and Houghton Mill. I was fascinated with the old Water Mill at Houghton, and Simon stayed at a good Riding Establishment where he was looked after splendidly. The next morning I rode off with a perfectly groomed cob.

It was always interesting to observe other people's hobbies; here on the flat lands there were Marinas galore.

I rode on through countryside new to me - rich arable lands, lovely wide grass verges in Leicestershire, and at last back to Derbyshire with its trails, then via the rough hill tracks of North Cheshire, and so back home.

Edith.

"James Herriot's Yorkshire."
1980

DATE   OVERNIGHT ACCOMMODATION

Aug 10 Mankinholes   Youth Hostel

Aug 11 Burnley   Friend

Aug 12 Dutton   Farm Guest House

Aug 13 Chipping   Friend's Farm

Aug 14 Slaidburn   Youth Hostel

Aug 15 Malham   Farm Guest House

Aug 16 Kettlewell   Youth Hostel

Aug 17 Horsehouse   Thwaite Arms

Aug 18 Aysgarth Fall   Youth Hostel

Aug 19 Grinton   Youth Hostel

Aug 20 Bellerby   The Cross Keys

Aug 21 Masham   Grange Country House Hotel

Aug 22 Carlton Minoit   Guest House

Aug 23 Thorpe-Under-Wood   Guest House

Aug 24 Harrogate   Pony Club Camp at Yorks Show Ground 5 Days

Aug 30 Pateley Bridge   Trekking Centre

Aug 31 Menston nr Ilkley   Riding School

Sept 1 Haworth   Youth Hostel

Sept 2 Mankinholes   Youth Hostel

This appears to be the only journey that Edith did not complete due to an accident. Her own horse was lame and I lent her my pony 'Kate'. Unfortunately the stable at Chipping had a sliding door, which Kate had never met before, and she pushed her way out of the stable, knocking Edith to the ground and causing her to cut her head on the concrete yard. Edith abandoned her ride and boxed home. The following is her planned route.

Aug 10

To Mankinholes.

Aug 11

Bridleway under Stoodley Pike dropping down to A646. Across road then up bridleway past Golf Course and along side of hill to go through wind farm onto Long Causeway and lanes and bridleways to Walk Mill and overnight.

Aug 12

By way of Fence and the Pendle Hills on lanes and tracks to Wiswell and Great Mitton to Hurst Green and Dutton.

Aug 13

Lanes and tracks to Chipping and ACCIDENT.

Aug 14

Lane past Leagram Hall Farm and bridleway through Lower Greystoneley and Higher Greystoneley, then lanes to Burholme Bridge and Langden Bridge to Dunsop Bridge, then right to Newton and B6478 to Slaidburn YHA.

Aug 15

B 6475 Tosside then left at chapel to Long Gill. Left to Hensley Hill and right to Rathmell. Turn left towards Giggleswick on lane, then right just before village to cross railway and A65 to Settle. Up steep hill and bridleway over Kirkby Fell to Malham YHA.

Aug 16

Lane past Malham Tarn to Arncliffe. Cross the river, then lane to Hawkswick and lane to B6160. Right to Kilnsey and cross river to Conistone, then lane to Ketttlewell.

Aug 17

Lane up steep hill to Thwaite Arms at Horsehouse.

Aug 18

Bridleway over moor to West Burton. Cross B6160 and lane to Aysgarth YHA.

Aug 19

Lane to Caperby, then right to Redmire. Left on lane over Redmire Moor to Grinton YHA.

Aug 20

From YHA up hill and over Cogdon Moor and army firing range. At X roads, left then right to Bellerby and Cross Keys.

Aug 21

A6108 then left into lane past South Dyke Farm to Cross Canes Farm, then right to cross A684, and keeping south cross river by church and onto A6108 to East Witton. South again on lanes and tracks then east to Ellingstring and lanes on to Fearby and Masham.

Aug 22

A 6108 to B6267, then lane to West Tanfield. Left onto A6108 and immediate left (before the river), and follow lane alongside river turning east to Wath and Middleton Quernhow. Cross A1 into bridleway for Skipton On Swale on A61, then bridleway through Coronation Whin to Carlton Miniott.

Aug 23

Bridleway to A167, then left after crossing disused railway, right into lane passing Salmon Hall to A67

Asenby. After village, left into lane to Poplar Hill and at Cundall, right to Norton Le Clay, then left to Boroughbridge. B6265, and then lane to Gt. Ouseburn and Thorpe Underwood.

Aug 24

Lane past Thorpe Hill Farm to B6265. Straight across into lanes for Whixley. The bridleway past High Farm, Wall's Close House and cross A1; then south to Coneythorpe and Flaxby. Right onto A59, then left to Goldsborough and bridleway to B6164. Right and cross river, then take lane alongside river to B6163. Left onto 'B' road then right through Forest Moor to Show Ground.

PONY CLUB CAMP.

Aug 30

Bridleway from Show Ground across railway to A61. Across road to bridleway and lanes to Daw Cross, past Hill Top Hall and Lind House, to cross B6162 to bridleway to Birk Cragg, then left and bridleway to B6161. Right then left to Barracks, then right to cross A59 to Hampsthwaite and Clint to B6165. Left to pass church, then lane on right to pass Well House and Fiddlers Green to Smelthouse and Wilsill, then lanes to Pateley Bridge.

Aug 31

Cross river going south on B6265, then left into lane towards Low Moor and bridleway over Flat Moor to High House Farm. Left into lane to Blubberhouses, right on A59 and left on lane to Askwith. Right to Ilkley, cross river and A65, cross railway and left onto 'B' road then right to Menston.

Sept 1

Via East Morton, Eldwick, Harden and Cullingworth, to Haworth YHA

Sept 2

To Mankinholes YHA

Sept 3

Home to Delph by one of usual routes.

"Yorkshire Journey."
1982

In 1981 Edith had shingles, so did not journey, but she was on her way again in 1982 determined to do the aborted 1980 ride. She kept a scrapbook of this ride and the notes under the route description are her own.

Aug 3

Delph to Denshaw, then Rough Hey lane to Rams Head (Th'Owd Tup) then Rapes Highway to Hollingworth Lake and Littleborough.

NOTES. 1st bridleway, Rough Hey Lane obstructed by old bedstead tied up with string. Mike, Maureen and Eileen have boxed over to ride home with me over the moor. Hollingworth Lake known as Weaver's Seaside.

Aug 4

Lane to Shore, the bridleway to Watergrove reservoir and north on Ramsden Road to Limersgate. Crossing A681 bridleway to Tower Causeway and down to A646. Left then right onto bridleway past Dean Farm and up hillside turning left on hill top to bridleway through wind farm and onto Long Causeway. Left then right onto bridleway to Hurstwood and lanes to Worsthorne, turning right to pass church into lane to High Halstead, Haggate and at

Golf Course left into Brierfield, crossing A56 to pass station and cross 2 rivers to Fence.

Aug 5

Lane past Stump Hall to Padiham, Higham then via Sabden and Nick Of Pendle to A59. Right and left into lane to Clitheroe.

Aug 6   REST DAY

NOTES   At launderette, washing from Waddow Guide Camp. International Clogger in town. Bawdlands - a cul-de-sac - lovely with flowers on edge of town on way to Edisford Bridge.

Aug 7

Lane crossing railway to West Bradford, then right and
left to Grindleton and on to B6478. Left onto 'B' road to Slaidburn.

NOTES   Fells in mist   Set out in cape. Lovely lane. Saw Heron.

Aug 8

B6478 to Tosside, then north on lane to Long Gill and Rathmell. On through Giggleswick, cross A65 and into lane to Stackhouse and Little Stainforth, to cross railway and join B6479 at Helwith Bridge.

NOTES *Long journey; rough and raining. Passed Mike Harding's House. Gypsy caravan and family going opposite way*

Aug 9 REST DAY

Aug 10

B6479 to New Inn, then Pennine Way over High Green Field to Beckermonds then lane North to Hawes

NOTES Met jockey who did some stitching for me. He rode for Peacock's Racing Stable and used to exercise Sheila's Cottage and Teal. Met yesterday's Nottingham Winner. Went back at night to meet jockeys who were surprised at my venture.

Aug 11 REST DAY

Aug 12

North on lane to cross river, then east through Askrigg to Aysgarth.

Aug 13

North on lanes to Caperby then east to Redmire and north over Redmire Moor to Grinton Lodge YHA.
Aug 14

B6279 Reeth then Arkengarthdale, to lane over The Strang, crossing A66 to B6277 to Barnard Castle.

NOTES   Met friends from 1976 ride. Mother and daughter ride. Kath and Leslie met me by car near Stake Forrest near end of long journey. Cancelled YHA and stayed with friends. Son is a beater on grouse moor.

Aug 15

B6277, then lane past Egglestone Abbey to A66. Left to Greta Bridge, then lanes to Barningham, Nesham, Kirby Hill, Washton to Richmond.

NOTES   Farmhouse B&B. Sam in loosebox, children's ponies in field. Farmhouse not easy to find. Late start next day.

Aug 16

B6271 to Brompton On Swale. B1263 to B6271 past Kiplin Hall, then lane and bridleway through Plumtree Moor Plantation. Right into lane to Streetlam and Danby Wiske.

NOTES: Wet and windy start and 18mile journey. Sam splendid loose box. Hostess husband jet pilot, co-pilot on brief holiday. Met young local falconer. Young walker arrived on coast-to-coast walk. Riders seem to do journey in half time. Nearby Scorton Village home of Cleveland Bays.

Aug 17

East on lane to cross railway and turn left on A167 then 1st right into lane to Brompton. Cross A684 to Bullamoor then left to A19 at Jeater Houses. Left and

1st right to Thimbleby and Osmotherly.

NOTES: Stayed with remarkable 72 year old man who breaks and trains horses and ponies Advised strong wind so missed part of Cleveland Way.

Aug 18

Lane south of Osmotherly going east to Chequers, then via Plane Tree Farm, Lane House Farm and Hazel Head Wood to Hawby.

Aug 19

South on lane then west to Boltby and Felixkirk. Bridleway to Hag House and Manor House. Cross A19 to South Kilvington. Bridleway across river and through Underwood Plantation to Woodhill Grange, then via Carr Plantation to lane and then to Carlton Miniott.

NOTES: Stayed with Doris who I met and became friends of the family on one of my earlier journeys. Their son Don boxed me to the Pony Club Camp. Doris's vet is James Herriot.

"The Great Circle."
1983

In 1983 Edith realised that after her attack of shingles in 1981 that she was coming to the end of her time as a long distance journeyer, so she planned to repeat her journey of 1979, but in the opposite direction, and visiting some of the places she missed out last time. The result was the journey she referred to as The Great Circle.

Unlike The Great Triangle, there was little publicity about this ride, and it was very much more low key than the 1979 ride. As a result there is no information about what happened, as Edith was not one to keep a diary or write down notes The only information is her itinerary sheet, and lines on her maps, with circles round villages passed through.

June 12

Via Greenfield and Mooredge Road to Brushes and Gallowsclough to Mottram, thence via Broadbottom to the hunt kennels as Charlseworth.

June 13

Monks Road to bridleway over Matley Moor and Lantern Pike to Birch Vale, then Sett Valley Trail to Hayfield.

June 14

Mount Famine bridleway to Peep O'Day and

bridleway to Brierly Green then lanes to Buxworth, Tunstead Milton and Combs.

June 15

Lane to White Hall Centre (Outdoor Pursuits) then Roman Road to A5004 to Buxton YHA.

June 16

Lanes to High Peak Trail and Royal Oak, Hurdlow.

June 17

High Peak Trail to Wirksworth.

June 18 REST DAY.

June 19

Lanes south to Shottle and A 517.

June 20

Lanes to Duffield and A6 South, then lanes via Edgehill to Little Eaton, Breadsall, crossing A608 then lanes via Stanley and Cat and Fiddle to A6096, then more lanes via Dale to Risley on B5010.

June 21 REST DAY.

June 22

Crossing A52 and M1 through Wilsthorpe to Sawley and following the Midshire Way signs from Sawley Marina via Ratcliffe on Soar and Gotham to Bunny.

June 23

Following Midshires Way signs via Bunny Woods to Old Dalby.

June 24

Lanes via Wartnaby and Saxalby to Asfordby to cross A6006 to Kirby Bellais and A607 thence by lanes via Great Delby to Leesthorpe.

June 25

Lanes via Somerby and Knossington to Brooke.

June 26

Lanes and tracks to Manton then lanes to Stamford.

June 27

Lanes to Warmington on A 605.

June 28

Lanes via Denton, and Glatton to Shawtry, then south on A1 to Whitehall then East on B1090 to Houghton at Huntingdon.

June 29

Via Hemingford Abbots and Hemington Greys across A1069 to Fenstanton, then across A604 to Conington, Dry Drayton, Madingley, Coton and Cambridge YHA.

June 30 REST DAY.

July 1

Lanes via Fulbourn across A1 to Balsham, then B1052 Linton across A604 continuing B1052 to Saffron Walden YHA.

July 2

Lanes Via Wimbush, Radwinter to B1053 and Great Stampford, then lanes to Cornish Hall End and B1057 to Little London, and lanes via Gainsford Hall to Castle Headingham YHA.

July 3 REST DAY.

July 4

To Colchester via lanes to Little Maplestead crossing major road, then lanes via Pebmarsh Chapel and Fordham to YHA.

July 5 REST DAY.

July 6

To Hatfield Heath via lanes crossing A12 to Silver End and A131 to Leez Lodge Lakes then A130 to Pleshey and B184 Hatfield Heath.

July 7 REST DAY.

July 8

Via B183 and lanes to Harlow Youth Hostel.

July 9 REST DAY.

July 10

Crossing A1019 to Roydon then lanes South to Broxbourne.

July 11

Lanes via Little Birkhamstead then crossing B158

to Cote Green and west through Welwyn Garden City crossing Ml to A6129 to Colman Green and Roman Road, then West again to cross A6 to Hatching Green and Redburn.

July 12 REST DAY.

July 13

Crossing A5 and Ml at Church End, West to Great Gaddesden, Little Gaddesden and north west to Ivinghoe YHA.

July 14 REST DAY.

July 15

Lanes bypassing Aylesbury going west and crossing A418 and A 413 to Quainton.

July 16/18 Bus to stay with friends.

July 19

Lanes to cross A41 to Ludgershall Brill, across B4011 at Oakley then via Studley, Beckley and Elsfield to cross A40 at Marston to Wolvercote, Oxford YHA.

July 20 REST DAY.

July 21

South on lanes to Harwell.

July 22

Lanes and Ridgeway Path to Streatley YHA.

July 23 REST DAY.

July 24

B 4009 through Aldworth, Hampstead Norris and cross M4 to Hermitage and Curridge.

July 25 REST DAY.

July 26/29

Lanes via Bagnor, Stockcross, Kintbury, Inkpen, Ham, Shallourne to stay with friends at Great Bedwyn.

July 30

Lanes crossing A338 to Oxenwood and Roam Road to Tangley, Clanville, Weyhill crossing A303 to

Abbotts Ann then across A343 to Longstock and Stocksbridge.

July 31 to Aug 2   Bus to stay with friends at Southsea.

Aug 3

Lanes South to Mottisfont and B3084, then lanes to Lockerley and A27 at Sherfield English. Lanes to Plaitford and across A36 to Landford Common and B3079 to Bramshaw.

Aug 4

Lanes East crossing B 3075 to Frogham.

Aug 5 REST DAY.

Aug 6

South on lanes to stay with friend at Ringwood.

Aug 7 REST DAY.

Aug 8

Lanes North West through Edmonsham to Cranbourne YHA.

Aug 9

Lanes via Gossage All Saints, Manswood, Tarrant Monkton, Tarrant Launceston to Tarrant Hinton.

Aug 10

Lanes via Tarrant Gunville, Sutton Waldron, across A350 to Childe Okeford.

Aug 11

Lanes West via Okeford Fitzpaine, Hazelbury, Kings Stag and across B3143 to Holwell and Holnest.

Aug 12/17 Bus to stay with friends in Yeovil.

Aug 18

Lanes via Yetminster and Stoford across A37 South of Yeovil to East Coker. Across A30 to Odcombe then across major road to Tintinhall. Across A303 to Ash then B3165 to Somerton and B3151 to Street YHA.

Aug 19

Lanes North passing Glastonbury then via North Wotton and Croscombe on A371 to Chilcote.

Aug 20

Lane North East crossing B3135 to A37 at Gurney Slade, then lanes east to Holcombe.

Aug 21

Lane North through Charlton crossing A362 to Wellow, Twinhoe and Millford.

Aug 22

Lanes North West across A367 to English Combe, Stanton Prior then across A39 to Burnett and B3116 to Keynsham. A4175 to Willsbridge via Upton Ceyrey to Wick and friends at Abson.

Aug 23 REST DAY.

Aug 24

North to Pucklechurch then East to Hinton Burton. North to Littleton and Alderton.

Aug 25 REST DAY.

Aug 26

Lanes via Sherston to Foxley and British Horse Society Member.

Aug 27 REST DAY.

Aug 28

Lanes via Shipton Moyne, Long Newton then east via Crudwell to Oaksey and north via Poole Keynes, Ewen, Coates to Duntisbourne YHA.

Aug 29

North on lanes via Colesborne, Dowdeswell, Whittington, Charlton Abbotts, Woodmancote and west via Bishops Cleeve and Stoke Orchard to cross M5 to Deerhurst, Walton, Lower Epperley and Course Wood Hill, to Staubton on A417 and friend.

Aug 30 REST DAY.

Aug 31

West via Redmarley D'Abitot and across M50 to Tillers Green and Much Marcle, Rushall, Checkley and friend.

Sept 1 REST DAY.

Sept 2

West via Mordiford to Hampton Dene at Hereford.

Sept 3

To guest house at Tupsey Hereford.

Sept 4

North on lanes via Sutton St. Nicholas and Bodenham crossing A417 to Risbury and Steen's Bridge.

Sept 5 To visit friend at Leominster.

Sept 6

North via Laysters Pole and Little Hereford to Ludlow YHA.

Sept 7 REST DAY.

Sept 8

Lanes north west via Bromfield, passing racecourse to Vernolds Common and Craven Arms.

Sept 9

Lanes north west to Longmynd and Bridges YHA.

Sept 10

Lanes North East via Church Pulverbach and Stapleton crossing A49 to Condover.

Sept 11

North east to Cross Houses and north to Atcham, crossing A5 to Uffington and B5062 to Haughton, then lanes to Upper Astley and across A53 to Astley and across A49 to Haston.

Sept 12

Lanes north to Clive, then east to cross A49 Preston Brocklehurst, and lanes to Stanton upon Hine Heath, then north to Hodnet.

Sept 13

Lanes east via Stoke Upon Tern, Wistanwick, Cheswardine, Doley and Bishops Offley to Eccleshall.

Sept 14

Lane north east via Sturbridge to A51 to cross M6 then lanes to cross A34 to Barlaston and friend.

Sept 15

Lanes north east to cross A520 onto B5029 to cross

A50 then lanes via Dilhorne to A521 and B 5053 to Ipstones.

Sept 16

Lanes and tracks via Waterhouses, and Calton to Ilam YHA.

Sept 17   Tissington Trail to Hartington YHA.

Sept 18

Tissington and High Peak Trail to Royal Oak, Hurdlow.

Sept 19

Lanes as on June 16 to Buxton YHA.

Sept 20

Via Millersdale, Wheston, Bradwell Moor and Pin Dale to Castleton YHA.

Sept 21

Via Hope and lanes to Yorkshire Bridge and Ladybower, then Strines and on to Langsett YHA.

Sept 22

Via Dunford Bridge and lanes to Ramsden Road bridleway to Ramsden reservoir, then via Holmebridge and Flush House to Harden Moss.

Sept 23

Via A635 to Wessenden Valley to Marsden, then via Standedge and Diggle home to Delph.

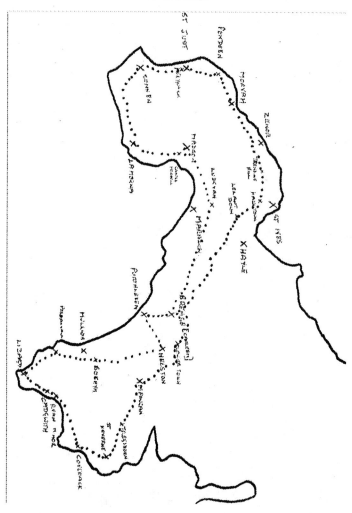

Cornwall 1984

"Cornwall."
1984

DATE	OVERNIGHT ACCOMMODATION		NOTES
July 14	Breage	Friend	Arrived a.m
July 15	Breage	Friend	Preparations
July 16	Breage	Friend	Hired horse
July 17	Breage	Friend	Horse grey mare
July 18	Goldsithney	Kennels	
July 19	Alverton	Penzance Youth Hostel	
July 20	Lamorna	Friend	
July 21	Rest Day		
July 22	Sennen	Wreckers Inn	
July 23	Sennen	Wreckers Inn	
July 24	St. Just	Youth Hostel	
July 25	Morvah	Farm Guest House	Went to theatre
July 26	Zennor	Farm Guest House	
July 27	Halstown	Trekking Centre	
July 28	Lelant Downs	Stables	
July 29	Breage	Friend	
July 30/31	Breage (Rest Days)	Friend	Washing and Prep.
Aug 1	Portleven	Farm Guest House	
Aug 2	Helston	Guest House	
Aug 3	Prendannack	Riding Stables	
Aug 4	Rest Day		
Aug 5	Ruan Minor	Guest House	
Aug 6	Cadgwith	Youth Hostel	
Aug 7	Coverack	Youth Hostel	
Aug 8	St. Kevine	Guest House	
Aug 9/10	Mawgom	Guest House	
Aug 11	Helston	Farm Guest House	
Aug 12	Breage	Friend	
Aug 15/16	Fowey		By Coach
Aug 17/18	Kingskerswell		By Coach
Aug 20/23	Yeovil		By Coach
Aug 24/26	Plymouth		By Coach
Aug 27	Delph	Home	'Yelloway' Coach

Whilst Edith kept a scrap book about Cornwall, this consisted of cuttings from leaflets on the area, and the only reference to her journey is a press cutting of her mounted on 'Bianca' when she took part in Halsetown Carnival dressed in her travelling gear as a Long Distance Rider. Whilst she did not win a prize, she was awarded a special certificate.

Unlike earlier maps there is no pencil line showing her route, just a few circles around the names of places she intended to pass through. The first ten day circle was ridden clockwise, the second anti clockwise.

On the first circle she circled or underlined Ludgvan, Madron, Castle Horneck, Lamorna Valley, Sennen, Kelynack, St Just, Pendeen, Morvah, Zennor, Trendine Hill, Halstown, Lelant Down and Carleen.

On the second circle she marked Porthleven, Helston, Bochym, Predannack, Lizard, Cadgwith, Ruan Minor Coverack, St Keverne, Lanarth, Tregidden, Mawgan and Lower Town.

From this limited information, it would appear that she stayed as close to the coast as possible.

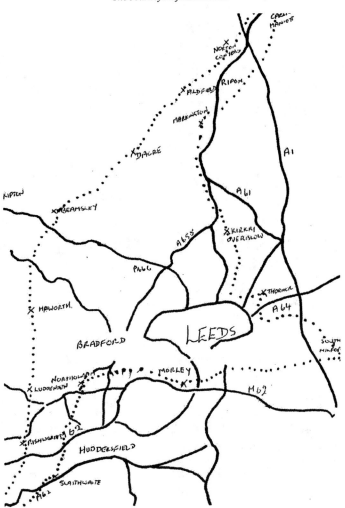

Across Yorkshire 1985

"Across Yorkshire."
1985

DATE	OVERNIGHT	ACCOMODATION
Aug 12	Slaithwaite	Bradshaw Riding School
Aug 13	North Owram, Halifax	Royd Farm Riding Centre
Aug 14	Morley	Relative
Aug 15	South Milford	Guest House
Aug 16	Thorner, Leeds	Westways Riding School
Aug 17	Kirby Overblow	Darroway Riding Centre
Aug 18	Rest Day	
Aug 19	Markington	Yorks. Riding Centre
Aug 20	Carlton Maniott	Guest House
Aug 21	Rest Day	
Aug 22	Norton Conyers	Guest House
Aug 23	Aldfield nr. Sawley	Farm Guest House
Aug 24	Dacre Banks	Youth Hostel
Aug 25	Beamsley, Ilkley	Farm Guest House
Aug 26	Haworth	Youth Hostel
Aug 27	Luddenden Foot, Halifax	Willow Royd Stables
Aug 28	Rishworth	Guest House
Aug 29	Home	

Aug 12

From Delph to Diggle and Diggle Hotel, then up
Boat Lane to Standedge and over top of cutting onto

bridleway over National Trust Land passing reservoir on left, then right and first left into Old Mount Road to A62 at Marsden. Straight across, passing church then right before railway and passing reservoirs, left under railway bridge to Heys.

Aug 13

Continuing north to A640, right then left into lane to Sowood Green. Left onto B6112 to Broad Carr, then lanes to Elland. Crossing river, then right and left into lane to Exley, then right into lane to Southowram and on to 'A' road. Straight across to Claremont, then lanes to Stump Cross, Dam Head and past hospital to Northowram.

Aug 14

Crossing A644 lanes through Coley and Norwood Green crossing A641 to Wyke and Oakenshaw. Across A638 and M606 to East Bierley, then across A650 to lanes past Ryecroft Farm then right past Park Wood and left to Tong. Bridleway to Cockersdale and across A58 to join B6126 across A62 and M621 to A643 Churwell (Morley.)

Aug 15

B6123 to Bantam Grove across A653 and under railway and through estate, skirting Middleton Golf Club, to Belle Isle, then bridleway crossing Ml to A61 past Rothwell Haigh Hospital to cross A639 to Woodlesford. Past Station to A642 and across river and canal then bridleway and lane to Astley and Allerton Bywater. Across A656 and lanes passing Newton Farm to Fairburn. Across A1, and lanes to cross A63 to Lumby and south Milford.

Aug 16

Lanes and bridleway past Lennerton Farm and sewage works to B1222. Right to Mattram Hall then left to Biggin and Partridge Hill. Left then right into Busk Lane past airfield to Ulleskelf. Left into Raw Lane to A162 then right to Limekiln Wood, then left to Sutton and Moor Lane to cross A64 and on to Bramham. Across A1 onto Roman Road and on to Thorner.

Aug 17

Lanes north past Barkers Plantation to East Rigton. Across A58 to East Keswick then north to cross A659 in to bridleway through Ox Close across river and past Paddock House. Cross lane and then bridleway to Lund Head and lane to Kirkby Overblow.

Aug 18 REST DAY

Aug 19

West on lane to bridleway crossing A61 at Swindon Lane Farm continuing on bridleway past New

York Farm crossing A658 to Horn Bank Farm across Nor Beck to lane. Right to Bunkers Hill then left and left again past Lund House then right to cross B6162 into bridleway through woods at Birk Crag and lane to Oakdale. Across B6161 then right past White House Farm, across A59 to Hampsthwaite, across river then right onto bridleway through Holly Bank Wood to Ripley Cross. B6165 into lane past Slate Rigg Farm then tracks and bridleway to lane at Hob Green to Markington.

Aug 20

East to A61 then left and right to lane and bridleway past Monkton Mains to Bishop Monkton. Left through village and lane to B6265. Right past racecourse to Bridge Hewick then left past Copt Hewick to cross A61 into lane to Hutton Conyers, Nunwick, Wath, Middleton Guernhow and across A1 to bridleway to Skipton on Swale, left at A61 then right onto bridleway to Carlton Miniott.

Aug 21 REST DAY.

Aug 22

North to bridleway past Carr Plantation then at Woodhill Grange left on lane. At Avenue Grange right into bridleway going north to join lane to South Otterington. Cross A167 and lane to Maunby. Bridleway crossing river and turning south to Pickhill.

Lane to Sinderby and across A1 on B6267 left to Berryhills and Sutton Howgrave and on to Norton Conyers.

Aug 23

South through Nunwick and Hutton Conyers to cross A61 to Copt Hewick. Right onto B6265 to Aldfield.

Aug 24

South to cross river then right past Sawley Hall and lane to bridleway to Summer Bridge and Dacre Banks YHA.

Aug 25

B6451 to Dacre then right into lanes to Long Ridge Crags and Thruscross Reservoir. Over Gill Moor to A59 and across to bridleway and tracks to Beamsley (Alternatively A59 to Beamsley.)

Aug 26

B6160 to Addingham. A6034 then left into lane over Nudge Hill to Silsden. Lanes to Kildwick, B6172 Glusburn and lane through Sutton in Craven to Laycock and on to Haworth.

Aug 27

Lanes to Upper Town then bridleway and tracks over Oxenhope Moor and Warley Moor via Hollin Hill to Luddenden Foot.

Aug 28

Lanes via Lumb to A58. Across into lanes to Rishworth.

Aug 29

A672 to Denshaw then home to Delph.

"Lake District."

I remember Edith planning this route to follow the route used by Robert Orrell and his two ponies, Thor and Jewel, in his book Saddle Tramp in the Lake District, published in 1979.

After talking to a number of her friends we all agree that this journey probably never happened, due to the terrain and condition of the bridle paths. Edith felt that, at her advanced age, it was unwise to ride a possibly difficult route.

Robert Orrell may well have written the route description for Edith as I know that she was in correspondence with him.

Barbara.

Friday

Drive to High Newton M6 Jnct 36 Take A591 then to 590 signed to Barrow. Turn right at Levene's Bridge, sign to Barrow then at Roundabout take A591 Meet at pub The Crown High Newton. Accommodation Grange~over-Sands.

Day 1 Sat July 1
To Torver Lunch Oxen Park   B&B Mrs Hyslop Torver Coniston

July 2   To Eskdale   Lunch   Newfield   Inn Seathwaite B&B Mrs Cook field outward bound

July 3   To Wastwater No lunch stop
B&B Wasdall Hall YHA

July 4   To Ennerdale   Lunch Wastwater Hotel
B&B YHA Ennerdale

July 5   To Gatesgarth Lunch Buttermere
B&B farm

July 6   To Langdale   Lunch Borrowdale
B&B Old Dudgeongill Hotel

July 7   To Coniston   Lunch Little Langdale
B&B YHA Far End, Coniston

July 8   To Lowick Green, Box Horses, Dine,
wine and drive home.

Day 2

Start at Torver on west side of Coniston Water. Take bridleway from Scar Head to join Walna Scar road to Seathwaite. Accommodation at Newfield Inn, perhaps for horses too. Plenty of Bed and Breakfast farms in area - I only know Ellwoods at Wallowbarrow Farm, tel. Broughton in Furness 492.

Day 3

Follow road from Seathwaite to Hall Dunnerdale, turn right at telephone box, cross road bridge and immediately over bridge turn right again to follow opposite bank of River Duddon to Wallowbarrow Farm.

Bridleway goes through farmyard and climbs by side of Wallowbarrow Crag to Grassguards then across open ground to gate in forest fence. Path continues round Harter Fell to foot of Hard Knott Pass near Brotherilkeld Farm. Harrison is the name of the farmer. Might accommodate you and horse. Tel. Eskdale 231. Will probably suggest alternative. If member of YHA Geoff Lee, Warden, Eskdale Youth Hostel is obliging and will accommodate horses - mention me.

Day 4

Ride down Eskdale to Boot. Go through hamlet, past Burnmoor Inn to gate next to Eskdale Mill. Through gate bear right up fell path for about 200 yards to another gate in wall. This is the old Corpse Road over Burnmoor, past Burnmoor Tarn to Wasdale. Mr. Graves at Wasdale Head Hall Farm will accommodate you and horses. Tel. Wasdale 245. Alternative- Wastwater Hotel (Youth Hostel)

Day 5

From Wasdale Head Hall follow path to National Trust Campsite. Bridleway leads through site to cross river and eventually join the road, Follow road to Wastwater Hotel. Go through hotel yard and follow path between river and farm next to hotel to gate at foot of Kirk Fell (Note: do not be tempted to cross hump backed bridge when leaving hotel yard.) Through fell gate then bear

Left up Mosedale and follow Black Sail Pass to

Ennerdale. Go past Black Sail Youth Hostel and follow track through forest to Gillerthwaite. Bob Orwell has ponies for rides and also takes guests in house, accommodation for horses - no phone in house.

Day 6

Follow forest track from Gillerthwaite along by Ennerdale Water to Whinns Farm and signpost showing bridleway to Buttermere by Floutern Tarn. Lovely bridleway as far as Floutern Tarn, and then descends to a wet valley. Bridleway crosses river at a gate in fence and then hugs the foot of Gale Fell till it meets Black Beck overlooking Crummock Water. Here the bridleway crosses the beck to descend on the north side of it. A gate in the fence is often wired up, but haul it away. Alternatively, on the south side of Black Beck a footpath descends to Scale Force and is to be preferred. Bridleway follows route by Crummock Water to cross Sour Milk Gill by Buttermere. National Trust gate across path sometimes chained but easy to lift off hinges. They have no right to block a bridleway. Lovely path continues rising slightly to the right. Don't be tempted by paths going left, but keep on wide stony path till you come to a gate opening onto fell. Follow path to Cratesgarth Farm. Lovely people, the Richardsons. Feed you and horses. Tel. Buttermere 256.

Day 7

Follow Honister Pass road to Borrowdale and picking up point at Seatoller car park.

Marvellous ride - hope you enjoy it.

"Dunford Bridge Circular."
1998
(Ref. To "Dobcross to Dudworth" 1948).

On the 29th and 30th July 1998 three riders set out to retrace Edith's steps to Dunford Bridge and back, on the return journey using bridleways which are fairly new and were not available to Edith on her journeys. She always had to return by the same route.

The three riders were: myself, riding Lydia - I knew all the route although I had never ridden it as a continuous journey; Pamela, riding Shah - it was practically all new to her; and Paul, on Faresh - he knew parts of the route having ridden them with me.

On a Wednesday morning we set out in pouring rain from Strinesdale, and by the time we reached the Roebuck, we were convinced that we were quite mad to continue for another 5 hours in what appeared to be a cloud burst. We reached Delph by way of Badger Edge and Hill Top Lane, then after passing through the village went down Hill End Road and across the A62 into Lark Hill Lane to turn left into Harrop Edge Lane which took us to Bleak Hey Nook, Wimberry Lee Lane, and the old track at the end took us to Standedge, where we crossed the A62 into the car park and took the bridlepath above the cutting to the National Trust Land and the track to the Marsden Road.

Right down the hill on the Marsden Road, still in pouring rain, then at the cross roads at the bottom, again right and up the hill to the track up the Wessenden Valley. This is much improved since Edith's time; the bridges over the ravines have been repaired and the whole bridleway, now definitive, is a joy to ride, except in pouring rain as we did.

At the top of the Wessenden Valley there is a car park, and behold, a catering double decker bus! FOOD. Hot drinks were consumed with thanks, and then off again, turning left onto the Isle of Skye Road, A 635, for almost exactly a mile. Then on the right, Springs Road and Nether Lane bridle paths passing Dingley Reservoir, then straight across at the cross roads to Flush House, where we bore right handed down the hill to Holmbridge.

Bearing right past the church we took the first left and then right at the 'T' junction to Brownhill reservoir and Ramsden Reservoir. At last it had stopped raining, but Lydia had lost a shoe. Never mind, press on. At the end of Ramsden Reservoir, left up the bridlepath through the trees, and at the 'T' junction left to Ramsden Road bridlepath to Copthurst moor.

At the macadam road we turned right and then we had the longest section of road in the whole of the first day At the 'T' junction where we turned right to pass Harden and Winscar Reservoirs, we missed a short bridleway which would have cut the corner, as we were trotting, and once again it was raining, so we had our heads down. At the 'T' junction after Winscar Reservoir we turned left for Townhead and the Western Trekking Centre where the horses were staying for the night.

Rocky made us VERY welcome, and the horses had a very nice field to themselves. Paul and Pamela stayed at the Stanhope Arms, whilst I went home for the horsebox and a replacement pony, Chips, who had been laid off for five months and had only had shoes on for two days. He loves this sort of work and trotted into the box with a look of sheer bliss on his face. Lydia was taken home, and at 9pm, I sat down to a hot meal.

Thursday morning, it was raining again, even harder than the previous day, I did not think that was possible, but it was. We tacked up the horses and set off through Dunford Bridge to the top of Woodhead. Here it was so bad that the horses just turned their backs to the weather and refused to go on until it stopped blowing such heavy rain into their faces. At the A628 Woodhead Road, one of the busiest roads I know, we went straight across to Salters' Brook. When the bridleway again reached the A628, straight across into the old byway, Longside. There is a concessionary route back down to the A628 with a straight across crossing with waiting spaces to the top of the Longdendale Trail at the Woodhead Tunnel end. This trail is part of the Trans Pennine Trail and runs for about 8 miles down the valley with only two minor roads to cross. About halfway down is the Torrside Visitor Centre with toilets and a catering van. At last it stopped raining and we had lunch. Chips was enjoying himself so much I had to stop him just galloping the whole way.

At Hadfield we went through the village on Station Road then at the roundabout left into Wooley Bridge Road, to the industrial Estate on the right The Transpennine Trail bears left here to Gamesley but we turned right through the factories, across the river then left through the barrier along a wooded track which comes out through another barrier into Water Lane. Right up Taylor Street, then at the A628 right and first left into Spring Street This passes a school and playing fields before becoming unmade. At the sharp right bend there is a track on the left which took us to

Dewsnap Lane and Roe Cross.

We went onto Motram Road, then immediately right into Gallowsclough Road. Passing through the farmyard, the gate out into the track behind the housing estate was difficult and Paul had to dismount, then we took a nice old lane to Brushes Country Park and the bridlepaths to Huddersfield Road, B6175. We went straight across into Grove Road and followed this to Wakefield Road, A635, where we went left and first right into John Street, which led us to Luzley Road, where we turned right. Although it had not rained since lunch we were all very wet and were pushing for home, so it was on to Mossley Road, A670, which we crossed into Broadcarr Lane. Shah had by this time lost a shoe, so we had to be careful to avoid stony tracks. Lane Head Road and Knowl Lane led us to the A669 at Lees Village where we crossed in front of the Red Lion, and by way of Victoria Street and Acorn Street got onto the old railway line, then down to the riverside bridlepath to cross the bottom of Dunham Street into Sidebottom Street, and across the A62 back to Strinesdale.

Each day we rode for about 5 1/2 hours excluding food stops. The ride was very enjoyable, except for the weather, and the horses coped very well, even Faresh, who had never done anything like this at all, and Chips who had been laid off for 5 months. Oh dear, the weather! It just poured with rain each day until about 2pm, when we were absolutely wet to the skin, even with good long Macs etc, it just went down our necks. Good fun, I will do it again. Many thanks to Rocky at the trekking centre for her hospitality.

"Shrewsbury Circle Revisited."
By mini caravanette
OCTOBER 1997
(Ref. To "Shrewsbury Circle" 1961).

Early in October 1997 I revisited the route Edith took in 1961. Bypassing Shrewsbury on the A 49, I travelled down to Leebotswood, where Edith had her lunch, probably at the Pound Inn. The A 49 is now a fairly busy road, but with grass verges most of the way. For present day horse riders, I would suggest that the start is made at Leebotswood.

Opposite the inn is a lane signed Woolstaston, which leads up hill to the pretty village with timber framed houses, then higher still to a cattle grid onto a moor land top, very reminicent of Edith's Pennines. A second cattle grid, then down a narrow leafy lane to Bridges Youth Hostel and village. DO NOT TAKE THE LANE PAST THE HORSE SHOE INN, a very pretty inn facing a stream, as this only leads past an ostrich farm up the hill to dead end at a dairy farm, instead bear right to the T junction then left to Norbury.

From Bridges to Bishop's Castle the route is narrow leafy lanes past pretty villages and farms through rolling countryside.

Bishop's Castle is a typical small market town with its cattle market. From there the A 488 has grass verges most of the way to Clun, or for the more adventurous with map reading skills, there are numerous narrow lanes all the way to Knighton, but there are not always sign posts at junctions, so take care.

At Knighton, turn right and pass the clock tower, the road signs are not very clear, and continue on the A488 as it climbs, a not too busy road, to a cattle grid and the Heart of Wales Riding School at the start of another stretch of moorland with wild ponies. Over another cattle grid, and down to Penybont and on to Rhayader.

At Rhayader there are three possible routes:

a) The A470, a long and winding route with great views, ideal for motors.

b) The white road parallel to the A470 to Llangurig, a pretty route for cycles and horses, past numerous farms. Both these routes join at Llangurig, a pretty villagewith a great church, then the A44 to Devils Bridge.

Devils Bridge is a local beauty spot with waterfalls imortalised by Wordsworth with a 30 minute walk taking in Jacobs Ladder. There are turnstiles with a £1 fee for entrance, and a 50p fee on the opposite side of the road. There is a car park and cafe, but no hitching rail for horse riding visitors.

The B 4343 to Tregaron is single track in places with high hedges and banks, very reminicent of Cornwall. I met these types of roadside hedges for most of the rest of the journey, and they were always well trimmed and cared for, much like someone's garden hedge. The route passed through a number of typical Welsh villages with their church and chapel, and typical Welsh farm houses.

Tregaron is a small Welsh town with many craft shops, art Galleries, potteries etc. There are also a number of cafes.

Tregaron to Talsarn was along the narrow winding

'B' road; for the more daring there are a number of White roads, but for me the 'B' road was narrow enough

From Talsarn to Llanarth the route was notable for the VERY steep and narrow Ystrad Aeron with the wonderful views from the top towards the coast at New Quay.

By now it was getting dusk, so I turned towards Synod Inn, then right towards New Quay, and found a caravan site to stay the night.

The following morning, I drove round New Quay in the pouring rain. It did not stop raining all day, and I was thankful I was in a caravanette, not on horse back in my usual manner.

From Synod Inn, I took the B4459, a narrow, twisting, and in places single track lane past numerous farms and villages with some wonderful small churches and chapels, in fact this tour could be called The Tour of Faith. The big surprise was finding a steamroller and workman's caravan parked outside a house in Pontshaen, obviously the home of a steam enthusiast. It is important here to follow the signs for Rock Woolen and Water Mill, as the road markings would send you, as they did me, the wrong way. I had to ask directions from two very wet horse riders, after finishing up in a farmyard.

The B4459 goes through Capel Dewi, with a great little church. I did not visit the Water Mill as it was raining so heavily, and on to the Industrial (well, one factory) village of Llanfihangel Ar Arth, from where a narrow white road leads to New Inn.

Straight across the A485 is a white road signed Brechfa, where Edith had pancakes, presumably at the superb little confectioners in the village. Between New

Inn and Brechfa is another moorland top with sheep and semi wild ponies, then a steep twisting lane through pine forests into the village.

From Brechfa to Llandeilo, I took the B4310 and A40, mainly due to the terrible weather causing the windscreen to mist up, and the wipers to work overtime, making map reading and driving difficult. If I had been on horse back or cycle with good maps in a map case, I would certainly have used the network of white roads through the many villages, but then I would have missed seeing the ruins of a castle on what appeared to be a man-made hill on the right hand side of the A40, at Dryslwn.

Llandeilo was the largest town I had seen since Leaving Shrewsbury, and it was obvious that this was where the locals did most of their shopping. In fact outside one village shop was a sign 'Use us or Lose us'.

At Llandeilo I took the A483 towards Ffairfach, and in the village turned left signed Bethlehem (I told you this could be called The Tour of Faith). On the right was a Craft Centre with car parking but no hitching rail. This lane again was narrow and twisting, but had wonderful views over Dyffryn Tywi. The river made great sweeps in the meadows.

Bethlehem school was one of the smallest schools I have seen, and a lane on the right leads down past farms with the ever-present high hedges to the A4069.

The A4069 is narrow with few verges and twisting through woods, but luckily it is also fairly quiet as there does not appear to be any alternative.

The left turn to Twynllanan is well signposted as is the turning to the youth hostel, but there the fun begins for motorists. This lane is VERY steep (1st Gear) narrow and twisting and in my opinion unsuitable for any motor vehicle except a 4x4 or farm tractor.

After a hair-raising two or so miles, which seemed to go on for ever, the Youth Hostel is hidden behind yet another old church. In fact, the only buildings are the church and Youth Hostel, which is an old Inn.

At the youth hostel I met a cyclist doing much the same route as myself, but in the opposite direction, and he gave me good information about the next few miles, and I gave him a bottle of milk. Leaving the Youth Hostel, take the lane at the side of the church, the other lane comes to a dead end at a gate. Great fun trying to turn round in a narrow lane with a stream at one side.

If I thought the way up was bad, the way down was a nightmare of narrow lanes with high hedges, tight bends and odd cambers. Please do not try this with anything bigger than a small car. The campervan I was driving was a Bedford Rascal, smaller than many cars.

With great relief I reached the minor road and turned right towards Trecastle, stopping at the first chance for a cup of nerve-restoring coffee. At Trecastle, a right turn onto the A40, then the minor road to Trallong. This would be a very pleasant lane for cyclists and horse riders, but another nightmare for cars, being VERY narrow with VERY high hedges, and EXTREMELY twisty. With my nerves shattered, I abandoned this lane for the A40, bypassing Brecon, then the A470. On cycle or horse I would have continued through Trellong and Aberyscir to B4519, then minor lanes to Felinfach and A470 then A438 and A479 to Talgarth; then over the mountain on the bridleways to Capel Y Ffin Youth Hostel.

I continued to Hay On Wye, the Town of Books, and its multiplicity of bookshops. The lane to Capel Y Ffin is well sign posted from the B4350 just before the town centre. The lane is single track with passing places, as it climbs and twists past woodland with bracken covered hills on one side up to a mountain top with plenty of picnicking areas. Unfortunately the mist was down; no, to tell the truth, we were in the clouds.

Dropping down over Gospel Pass (the Tour of Faith again), the cloud lifted to reveal wonderful views. The youth hostel was perched on the hillside below the bridle path. I turned round to retrace my steps to Hay On Wye and met a flock of sheep being brought down the lane by the farmer aided by an ATV and sheep dogs. On the mountain top was a herd of semi-wild ponies.

Returning to Hay-on-Wye, I took the road through Clifford, with its ruined castle, to the toll bridge. There is a 50p toll to cross for most users, but no posted fee for horses. I don't suppose they get many. The bridge is wooden and could cause problems for some horses.

I turned right onto the A438, with its wonderful old houses, many of them half-timbered and very ancient. The road was reasonably quiet and had a verge; then left to Eardisley, a truly superb black and white village on the Black and White Trail.

The lane to Lyonshall was well signed and ran past rolling farmland and pretty farms and cottages into the village, and then the A44 for a short distance and left onto lanes to Shebdon, and still more lanes through Lingen. Good map reading is necessary here as the lanes are narrow with many side turnings, but it is worth it for the numerous 16th, 17th.and 18th century houses, farms and barns. Then on to Knighton, a town of Victorian and Edwardian villas.

By now it was getting quite late, and dusk was falling so I took the A4113 then the B4367 to Craven

Arms. It was now 6.30 and going dark, so I refuelled and set off up the A49 hoping to see signs for a campsite. At Church Stretton I called a great chippy for fish and chips, then returned to the A49.

As I never did find a campsite, I returned home to Oldham arriving home at 10.15pm having been driving for almost 12 hours.

"Hadrian's Wall Revisited."
1997
(Ref. To "Northumberland And Durham." 1977)

Having ridden from Oldham to Howarth on my pony in June 1997 I decided to start this journey in my faithful 'Bambi' caravanette at Howarth

Taking the B6143 out of Howarth towards Keighley I followed an urban road to Slaymaker Lane on the left. This became more rural, passing farms until it became a 'T' junction with what appeared to be an old chapel converted into apartments. In this part of the country numerous old mills and chapels are being converted into very high-class flats. Slaymaker lane is a pretty wooded lane with ivy covered stone walls.

At the 'T' junction, straight across into Slack Lane, which twists and turns, at times a single track at others wide and open, passing numerous farms of typical Pennine construction. At the next 'T' junction, left and pass some quarries with strange towers and obelisks. There are a number of paths through the heather to the hill top, and this is an ideal picnic stop with the superb views over the valley of Sutton in Craven.

At the main road, right and first left down a narrow lane 'Lane Ends Lane', to the 'T' junction where a right turn gives wonderful views of yet another valley and hillside resplendent in autumn colours. The left turn is very sharp and drops down to cross the river before climbing steeply to a 'T' junction. A left turn then left at the cross roads brings you into Lothersdale, a typical Dales village of old stone houses with its village pub.

Through the village and out into the countryside

and after a sharp left bend turn right at the grass triangle to pass the radio masts on your left. Right at 'T' junction and over a cattle grid then immediately left down to Elslack. Just over the cattle grid are parking areas where I stopped for a brew and to admire the view.

Elslack is a very pretty Dales village with ancient cottages and houses and a village green. Here there is an offset cross roads, where I turned right then left down a lovely lane with pheasants crossing the road; in fact one cock ran in front of me for about 50 yards until he flew onto a fence.

Rounding a bend Broughton Hall gates were on my right, a fabulous old house converted into a business park, and the view up to the river here was incredible.

I then met the A59, a horribly busy road, but luckily there were only about 100 yards to travel before the left turn to Gargrave. The village of Broughton was full of picturesque cottages and the chapel had been converted into a very nice home, but this lane to Gargrave was one of the busiest on the journey

At Gargrave I turned right onto the A65 - another very busy road, but a short distance brought me to the turn for Cracoe and Lynton. About a mile up this lane was a 'Y' junction with the old hall in the fork. I took the right branch and followed the winding, sometimes steep, lane past the village inn, the 'Angel Inn' at Hetton where I spoke to two ladies who were very interested in what I was doing and Edith's journeys. This is an area of rolling countryside and stone villages where even the bus stops are stone built with flag stone roofs. The stones walls around Cracoe are white, reminding me of the White Peaks of Derbyshire.

Cracoe is a busy village where I turned left onto the B6265 and followed it past the stone quarries (during the week there are probably numerous large lorries in the area) to a right turn opposite the main gates of the quarry. This led to Lynton, my favourite village on the journey. The village green was bounded by the tree-lined road, a river with an ancient bridge and ford, the Fountaine Hospital Chapel and the Fountaine Inn with other stone cottages nestling behind them. Truly a village to dream of.

Straight across the B6160 and on to Grassington which everyone has heard of. If time allows it is well worth a visit, but I was on a tight time scale, two days to do a journey that deserved four.

Left at Grassington and past the police station to follow a winding lane through Wharfdale with great views over the river, dales houses and villages and tree-lined, mossy wall-lined lanes. Passing through Conistone I kept on the lane to Kettlewell. The reds and greens and golds of the autumn trees were a sight for sore eyes. But a word of warning: this lane was NOT suitable, for large motor homes or caravans.

From Kettlewell, I took the B6160 to Buckden. Along this road are numerous old farms and barns with the 'through stones', the Yorkshire form of wall ties, and outside stone steps.

At Buckden I branched left into Langstrothdale. This is a river valley with steep sides and rocky river bottom There were many cars and families enjoying a day out in this valley Take time to stop and overlook the hamlet of Yockenthwaite, before passing through Deepdale and starting the long climb up to the moor top and the highest road in Yorkshire

Yes, that road sign did say 1 in 4. Believe it, and

engage low gear. With my ears popping, I crept down the hill. It felt like going over the top on the big dipper as I dropped down the Hawes and the Wensleydale factory shop and Visitors' Centre.

At Hawes I turned right onto the A684 then left for Thwaite, climbing up over some of the most inhospitable moorland I have seen. Snow poles bounded the road to keep foolhardy winter travellers onto the macadam and off the peat. The hills were steep and winding and I was thankful that the weather was sunny.

From Thwaite I took the B6270 all the way to Kirkby Steven. Do not let the 'B' Classification fool you. This is a winding country road, in places narrow and after Keld it goes through a cliff-hung valley with waterfalls, and then climbs up to a black peat bog moor before dropping by way of a number of very steep, including 1 in 4, hills down to Nateby. The steepness of the road can be judged by the fact that I met large numbers of hang-gliders leaping off the cliff faces alongside the road.

At Nateby the B6259 leads into Kirkby Steven, where I joined the Cumbria Cycleway. The signs for the cycleway are badly faded, and the turning out of Kirkby Steven, a market town worthy of a stop, is signed to the Auction Mart.

The route then took me through twisting rolling lanes, through stone villages with village greens, and pubs, usually next door to the church; and on to the market and Horse Fair town of Appleby In Westmorland, with its red stone houses, market place and river. Do stop if you can.

Follow the road signs for Dufton, a village of red stone and painted cottages. Under Dufton Dyke, watch out for the pheasants and rabbits in the road or you will be having them for supper. Plan a short stop at the village of Skirwith, perhaps for a meal at the village pub, or fresh baking from the bakery. At Ousby, watch out for the turning for Melmerby and the A686, it is easy to miss.

It was now getting late on my first day, so I pushed on up the A686 as it twisted and climbed over moorland to 1903 feet at the summit, where there is a cafe with plenty of parking. The road then dropped steeply into Alston where there was a return to the softer cattle country from the hard high sheep country I had just driven over.

A left onto the A689 and rolling countryside in the gathering dusk to Lambley and camping just outside Haltwhistle.

The South Tyne Trail runs between Alston and Haltwhistle. Parts of this trail were opened in early 1997 with further sections due. This is a wonderful route and it would be worthwhile contacting Northumberland County Council to see if it could be used. Very little was available to me.

Sunday morning at 7.30a.m. found me walking on the South Tyne trail which runs from Laiston to between Lambley and Haltwistle. I found it disconcerting to find it way-marked as a footpath whilst the legend on the information board seemed to show it as a bridleway, (a series of dots and dashes).

After breakfast, I set off in bright sunshine to Haltwistle. The A69 is now a high-speed bypass, but luckily I only used it for about 100 yards, and there was a cycle path and grass verge all the way. Haltwistle itself is worthy of a stop, but I found it difficult to navigate, but following the signs for

Hadrian's Wall put me on the right route.

I had now climbed out of the sunshine and was travelling in varying amounts of mist. This was to continue all day, with the mist on the hilltops being very thick, and I did not finally leave the mists until I returned to Kettlewell in the late afternoon.

Bardon Mill and the Visitor Centre are well signed from the B6138, but I have to admit I never saw Hadrian's Wall. It was just too misty, and I was in too much of a hurry. The Visitor Centre has a Pay and Display car park costing £1 and the Centre itself is open 9.30 –5pm and houses Tourist Information, Toilets, Shop etc. It was still not open when I called so onwards toVinolandia, which I had been recomended to visit by a gentleman in Thwaite. This has a free car park with picnic areas, but it is about 1 mile from the road down a narrow lane with passing places, not recommended for caravans. The entrance charges for the museum, excavation site etc in 1997 was £3.50 adults £2.90 OAP and Student and £2.50 a child. Dogs are not allowed through the turnstiles. This is a site well worth a visit, but again I was too early.

At the A69 1 turned right, then bypassed Bardon Mill to take the next lane to cross the A686. The A69 was extremely busy even at 9.45a.m. on a misty Sunday morning, but most of the roads and lanes in this area have grass verges of varying use due to drainage ditches.

The B6295 wound its way to Catton and on to Allendale, where on the outskirts it divides, and I took the right fork to a pub and the right turn to Ninebanks and Carrshield. The lane twisted and turned between walls or hedges through rolling countryside with stone houses and farms to Carrshield, where I found a great cafe serving homemade cakes and food. This was attached to the School House Gallery, an art gallery with a few antiques. As a lover of Victorian watercolours for me this was a real find.

Ninebanks has an old tower, which appears to be the remains of a fortified house and between Ninebanks and Carrshield is The Hole Priory, a Buddhist Monastery. I met a number of monks walking the lane.

After Carrshield the lane starts to rise, passing the remains of old quarries until it reaches the moorland top and at the highest point I left Northumberland, and dropped down to Nenthead.

In Nenthead I took the lane on the left signed for the Heritage Centre with its play areas and cafes, then passing through the old village I took the steep lane on the left up the single track road over moorland and through woodland to join the B6277.

I followed this 'B' road all the way to Barnard Castle. This road goes over high moorland with farmhouses crouching in the valley bottoms and on the left below Forrest in Teesdale is the car park for High Force Waterfall. There are toilet facilities here.

At Bowlees, a short distance away, is a Visitor Centre with cafe and toilets run by the local ranger service, and it was here that I met a ranger whose mother had run the Youth Hostel at Langdon Beck and he remembered Edith being there on her journey when he was a youth.

At Middleton In Teesdale I decided to take the B6278 to Barnard Castle as I wished to see more of the town than 1 would have done on the B6277. The top part of the town has Edwardian and Victorian stone villas, and then I came to a typical market place with many small and interesting shops. Lower down the hill the houses become older with a number of interesting early 18th Century buildings, and round the corner on the hill overlooking the river and bridge are the ruins of the castle. I must revisit this town with more time to spend.

Immediately over the bridge the B6277 continues to the A66, a horrid road, but only 300 yards before a left turn towards Reeth, a switchback of a road crossing upland farmland and over a high moortop in heavy mist, following the signs to Reeth and dropping down to Arkengarthdale.

Reeth is a fabulous town with a Folk Museum, shops, Yorkshire Dale Centre etc., well worth allowing time to visit. I left following the signs for Leyburn and after crossing the river took the lane on the right towards Leyburn.

The lane climbed steeply to a moorland top, where there were signs 'Danger ARMY FIRING RANGE'. The mind boggles, Further on were more, signs 'ARMY TANK DRIVERS UNDER INSTRUCTION'. Imagine meeting one of those. Who gives way?

At this point I decided to cut the corner and miss out Bellerby and go on to Leyburn. I was glad I did as it turned out to be a lovely market town with many interesting shops not the least of which were the Teddy Bear Shop, and the Fudge Shop where I bought some great fudge.

Passing the market place I took the A684 through Wensley, a gorgeous ancient Dales village and, after crossing the river, took the lane on the left signed Carlton and Coverdale.

It was in Carlton that I saw my first red telephone box and realised that all through this journey, I had seen phone boxes every few miles and none of them vandalised.

Horsehouse turned out to be no more than an inn, a church and a few houses, then the lane became even narrower and twisted its way between Dales farms to a high moorland top. The views were probably splendid, but I was in a thick mist and had enough to do following the road and avoiding the sheep. There were innumerable cattle grids on this section until the lane started to drop into Kettlewell.

BELIEVE the sign that is a 1 in 4, or steeper, with a tight 'S' bends with strange cambers. I was in second gear and frightened to death. DO NOT TRY THIS ROAD in anything bigger than a car. Personally I will never go down it again except on my own two feet. I would rather go on the 'Big One' at Blackpool, and I won't go on that either.

At the bottom I pulled in to let my brakes cool. The Bambi had not let me down. Then on to Kettlewell. The other hills did not seem half so intimidating. I would have loved to have stopped, but time was pressing. So on to the B6160, which is a fairly busy road.

The second lane on the right (not the one through a gate) leads to Arnecliffe, a pretty village of 18th Century cottages round a village green, (Emmerdale was once filmed there) then up a narrow, white walled lane over Darnbrook Fell to Malham Tarn. This is a 'honey pot' beauty spot, and then to Malham, a pretty village with a river running through, toilets and shops.

More lanes, softer now, led back to Gargrave, and I retraced my steps through Lothersdale to Howarth and Hebden Bridge, where I took the A646 to

Mytholmroyd. Cyclists and horse riders can take bridleways to Withens Clough Reservoir, then a pretty lane to Cragg Vale. As I was in the 'Bambi' I took the B6138 to Cragg Vale then continued up the road to the A 58.

I turned right down to Littleborough and made my way home via Rochdale

AN ARTICLE FOR THE BRITISH HORSE SOCIETY

By EDITH BOON

This is the story of how a childhood dream came true, which led to serious thinking about the importance of the Rights of Way movement, especially where riding is concerned.

When I was seven years old, long before I rode a horse, I had a great desire to undertake a long journey on horseback, which would enable me to visit many of my friends and relations in different parts of our delightful country. This dream was realised at the age of seventy. I did not learn to ride until I was twenty-five years old and only succeed in buying my own horse at the age of thirty-five. I was an urban area child. Now, more and more of these non-privileged children, with their parents' help, become riders and even pony owners.

This stage could be entitled "In Praise of Parents", for in my childhood my parents, perhaps unwittingly, fostered my desire by teaching me to love the countryside. My mother helped me to label my collection of pressed wild flowers and father could tell me the names and habits of the birds. He was also a "stickler" for using Rights of Way. We must not trespass, and so in our rambles we had to read maps in order to find our way about legitimately. Throughout these childhood walking days I daydreamed that I was travelling the tracks on horseback. I don't suppose my parents or my two younger brothers knew this.

Throughout my teenage days I walked and walked, still using maps to help my Rambling Club to plan attractive journeys over our local boggy-topped Pennines. Now I am Chairman of the West Pennine Bridleways Association, which is running hard, but not fast; local authority wheels grind so slowly!

As soon as I had a horse of my own, I spent all my spare time riding tracks around my home, and at holiday times my cob and 1 would set out, sometimes with friends, on journeys which lasted one or two or three weeks. Mostly we started the journey directly from home, sometimes using a railway horsebox to start out a little further afield. My now famous long distance ride, much publicised by the media, was only my twenty-second holiday journey. I merely viewed the three months' venture as an extension of the pattern followed so many times before. It was my custom to spend, and enjoy, a great deal of time planning before I set out, so my horse was assured of accommodation every night, just as I was!

When "The Great Triangle" ride from home (Delph, a village in the Pennines half way between Manchester and Huddersfield) to Yeovil to Colchester, to home, is being discussed, with my tongue in my cheek, I tell the tale of the 'Lucky Sevens', for I was very lucky throughout my journey, even weather wise! At seventy years old - retired of course - I said to myself, "It is now or never". My father had a theory that one felt very different every ten years. He had never felt tired until he was seventy. My plans developed. It turned out that I would set out on June 17th and return home on September 17th. I would spend my seventieth birthday on the seventh day of the seventh month at Burley Gate, near Hereford. There I was splendidly feted. Although the journey was to take 93 days allowing for rest days and sight seeing days etc., I would sleep in seventy-two beds! So now, when folk insist on my telling them how many miles I rode, I say seven hundred and seventy seven miles!

On my daily journeys, I used bridleways and miles of English lanes, meandering through the world - famous variety of English country scenes. It proved to be an epic journey; because of my age, and the distance to be covered, the media took a great interest. Almost daily I was interviewed and photographed by the Press, Radio and T.V.

In travelling about to talk to a variety of societies about the journey, I have found that people are very interested in my planning. It is my custom to set up a "Route Sheet" many months before setting out on any journey. The dates are written in columns and opposite each are recorded the details as they are fixed up. Imagine how the Post Office profits by my schemes! Separate letters are often necessary when booking my cob's accommodation. I collect and note information about the suitable places for map exchanges, I note receiving points for clean clothes parcels, and the possible places for re-shoeing. I must be near a village post office on a Thursday, for that is pension day! The women in my audiences certainly enjoy my account of the clothes washing plans. I use three sets of riding gear, one on me and two on the move. In 1979 I made use of launderettes in the small towns, but where convenient I leaned heavily upon my very kind hostesses. There was a time when I could trust the speed of the post. I would put my dirty clothes in a brown paper parcel and send them to my friend at home, who would wash them immediately, and all she had to do to return the clean clothes to the correct place was to turn the brown paper inside out, for I would have put the forwarding address on the inside.

My resting places are quite near together for I organised daily distances very carefully. The morning ride, very roughly, is determined by a time limit; that is to 2.5 hours at 3 mph., so roughly a seven miles journey. My journeys were never intended to be marathons. Lunchtime is deemed very important, for the horse must have two hours grazing, which also allows for the removal of all gear, and the mount is then given a chance roll. Sometimes a stable is found and I am delighted with the provision of a meal of corn, and some hay. Sadly, at one or two midday points on the last journey tethering was the only choice for resting and a "bought" loaf the only food. I would move on as soon as possible in this case to reach a happier situation for the horse. The whole long journey was organised on an average of fifteen miles per day only. Grazing is the rule, and stables are very welcome, but few and far between.

My night stops vary considerably. I use Youth Hostels to form a basic pattern. These are comfortable and reasonably priced with attractive food, planned usually by the very worthy wardens' wives. Friends and relatives provide a very happy and helpful part in filling in my lists. I must spend much time studying lists of accommodation sent to me by Information Bureaux. Publicity, through my friend who is a free-lance journalist, brings many most attractive invitations, and the rest of the spaces are filled with guesthouses or farmhouse accommodation. I am pleased to use riding establishments if I can. It can all be quite expensive and the horse usually requires £1 per night for grazing, and for stabling, sometimes £5, with often 50p for midday grazing.

One of the strongest features of my tours is the outstanding kindness and helpfulness of people! Travel educates and my mount always learns how to "ogle" the farmers.

Folk who ride themselves, and generously invite me to stay in their homes and my horse in their stables, are very understanding. It is impossible to tell in an article how much they help. Mrs Barker of Foxley introduced herself to me by 'phone as I progressed on the last long ride. She described how I could meet her and her four-legged companion on a bridleway, which was the old Roman Road, "The Fosse Way". She led me to her home and gave Simon and me a great deal of help. The details of numerous similar situations cannot be told in one article, but must wait for a possible book to be written in the future

Edith never did write her book.

Barbara Haigh was born in 1941 in Oldham to cotton mill working parents. She started riding in 1956, when she first met Edith Boon.

When Edith founded the Saddleworth Pony Club, Barbara was a founder member and later became a founder member of Oldham and District Riding Club. She is a long-standing member of West Pennine Bridleways, taking over as chairman on Edith's death.

She is the British Horse Society County Access and Bridleways Officer for Greater Manchester, and for many years has been a riding member of the Endurance Horse and Pony Society.

She is a committed 'grass roots' rider of 'grass routes'.